MUTUAL FUNDS

YOUR KEY TO SOUND
FINANCIAL PLANNING

MUTUAL FUNDS

YOUR KEY TO SOUND FINANCIAL PLANNING

LYLE ALLEN

AVON BOOKS ◆ NEW YORK

MUTUAL FUNDS is an original publication of Avon Books. This work has never before appeared in book form.

This book is intended to provide general information about mutual funds. The publisher and author cannot assume responsibility for individual decisions made by the reader and cannot be held responsible for any losses which may result because of information contained herein.

Text on pages 28–31 reprinted with permission of Investment Company Institute. For more information, write 1401 H Street NW, Washington DC 20005.

AVON BOOKS
A division of
The Hearst Corporation
1350 Avenue of the Americas
New York, New York 10019

Copyright © 1994 by Lyle Allen
Published by arrangement with the author
Library of Congress Catalog Card Number: 94-11923
ISBN: 0-380-77690-1

Library of Congress Cataloging in Publication Data:

Allen, Lyle.
   Mutual funds: your key to sound financial planning / Lyle Allen.
      p.   cm.
Includes index.
1. Mutual funds.   2. Investments.   I. Title.
HG4530.A5   1994   94-11923
332.63'27—dc20   CIP

First Avon Books Trade Printing: December 1994

AVON TRADEMARK REG. U.S. PAT. OFF. AND IN OTHER COUNTRIES, MARCA REGISTRADA, HECHO EN U.S.A.

Printed in the U.S.A.

OPM   10   9   8   7   6   5   4   3   2   1

Contents

Introduction

No question about it, the 1990s should be a profitable time for investors. In the 1990s, investors will have many opportunities to make money and achieve their financial goals.

Whether you are a beginner or an experienced investor, this book can help you profit from investment opportunities and reach your goals, whatever they are. If you want to save for the down payment on a house, provide for your children's college, supplement retirement, or put aside money for something else, this book can help you.

The best way to get a head start on your goals is to have an investment plan. This book shows you how to evaluate your current financial situation and develop such a plan. If you already have a plan, this book will help you determine whether it is adequate to reach your goals.

The theme of this book is that mutual funds should be included in most investors' financial plans. Although several types of mutual funds are available, open-end, no-load growth funds are specially emphasized. They offer a convenient way to invest, and many provide a good return on investors' money.

The mutual fund industry has grown through the years into a $2 trillion business with over four thousand funds. They employ professional managers, require a relatively small amount to open an account, and provide an array of shareholder services. An attractive feature of mutual funds is that federal and state laws regulate what they can and cannot do with investors' money. Funds must make a thorough disclosure of their operations to the Securities and Exchange Commission, state regulators, and their shareholders.

This book shows you how to invest in mutual funds using the Dollar-Cost Averaging Plus (DCAP) formula. This new and easy-to-use formula is a successful way to invest in funds. It requires that you invest monthly and that you vary the amount of your investment in relation to a target price. The formula can greatly increase the return on your investments in a fund.

You will learn about the advantages and disadvantages of investing in mutual funds; where to get information on funds and how to select funds for investment; how to invest in stocks as well as funds; where and how to open a brokerage account and possible pitfalls; and how to assess annuities, rental real estate, limited partnerships, bonds, and other investments.

You will be shown how to tie everything together in a total financial plan that has direction, priorities, and the potential to produce a sizable nest egg for your special goal.

This book is primarily for the person who wants to manage his or her own investments without the help of full- service stockbrokers, insurance agents, or financial planners. Managing your investments isn't easy, but it can be very rewarding. It requires time, patience, and, most of all, a desire to succeed.

Before You Invest

Few people would drive to New York without first looking at a road map to determine the best way to get there. You should apply the same principle before you invest. It's to your advantage to identify your goals and develop a road map or plan before you make any investment decisions.

You can set goals, develop a plan, and reach investment decisions yourself, without the use of a full-service broker, insurance agent, or financial adviser. Keep in mind that anyone who provides help on your finances will charge for the service, usually a very steep charge.

SETTING GOALS

The most successful investment plans are those with a sense of purpose—a goal. Unless you have worthy goals to achieve, your plan lacks direction. You probably can't afford all your goals at once, so decide which are most important and work to achieve them first.

What is a worthy investment goal? It involves saving for a future event that has a realistic objective and a dollar amount. Some of the more popular goals are:

- Save for a major purchase.
- Save for a vacation.

- Provide for your children's education.
- Save for the down payment on a house.
- Supplement your retirement income.

List Your Goals

Make a list of your goals, how much they are going to cost, and the date you expect to achieve them. The cost of some goals may be difficult to assess, because taxes, inflation, and unexpected emergencies will affect your financial situation over the years.

If your goal is to invest to pay for college expenses, for example, estimate the total amount you will need. To arrive at that estimate, you will have to make assumptions such as the increases in tuition costs, the rate of inflation, and increases (or decreases) in your family's income. You must also decide on the investment risk you feel comfortable with, and calculate the amount you need to save monthly to reach your goal.

After you list your goals, classify them as either short-, medium-, or long-term. This distinction is important because it determines which securities to include in your investment plan.

Short-term Goals

Short-term goals are the ones you want to attain rapidly—in less than five years. They could include the down payment on a house, a vacation, or a major purchase.

If you have some of the money you need for your short-term goals, consider investments that are not highly speculative. There is no reason to jeopardize the money you already have by making risky investments. Investments such as government securities, high-quality bond funds, and money market mutual funds are ideal for short-term goals. With all short-term investments, make certain their maturity date coincides with the date of your goal.

If you have no money set aside for your short-term goals, consider investments that are more speculative. These include common stocks and growth mutual funds.

Medium-term Goals

With medium-term goals, you have more time and investment choices. Maybe you'd like to buy a larger house or a new car in about five or six years. Since these goals are a few years away, you could hold conservative as well as speculative investments. Investments suitable for medium-term goals are growth mutual funds, bond funds, and common stocks. As the date approaches when you will need the money, sell your stocks and mutual funds and put the proceeds in a money market mutual fund. There is no need to continue with more speculative investments as your goal draws near.

Long-term Goals

Long-term goals usually cost the most and take several years to attain. They could include funds for college for your children, money to supplement retirement, and money for a second home. Since these goals are years away, you can be more speculative with your investments. Growth funds, common stocks, and zero-coupon bonds are good investments for long-term goals.

MONTHLY INCOME AND EXPENSES

Once you decide your goals and the time to reach them, review your current financial situation. To do that, complete the monthly income and expenses worksheet below. The worksheet contains two parts. The first part is for listing basic living expenses—those that are essential and necessary. The second is for listing discretionary items—those that are nonessential and can be reduced or discontinued. The worksheet doesn't have to include exact figures. Rather, it should be a general accounting of your monthly income and expenses. After you complete the worksheet, you will be able to:

- Determine your monthly living expenses.
- Decide which discretionary items you can cut back on or drop.
- Determine how much money is available for investments after you pay your bills.

MONTHLY INCOME AND EXPENSES WORKSHEET

(A) LIVING EXPENSES		(B) DISCRETIONARY COST ITEMS	
Housing (mortgage, rent)	_____	Credit cards	_____
Utilities (electric, gas, water, phone)	_____	Clothing	_____
Food	_____	Personal care (barber, beauty parlor, cleaners, cosmetics)	_____
Medical expenses	_____	Books, newspapers, magazines	_____
Insurance (life, health, auto, house, rental)	_____	Transportation	_____
Other	_____	Travel	_____
		Education	_____
		Entertainment	_____
		Gifts	_____
		Other	_____
Subtotals: (A)	_____	(B)	_____
Monthly net income	_____		
Less total of columns A and B	_____		
Money available for investing	_____		

Reducing Living Expenses

The most obvious benefit of the monthly income and expenses worksheet is that it shows you where your money is being spent. In addition, it can help you reduce your monthly expenses and locate money for investments. You may be surprised at how much your expenses can be cut if you really try.

Look at your living expenses in column A on the worksheet. Go over the items to see if you can reduce them. Here are some ideas on how you can make reductions.

• Housing. If you have a house mortgage, see whether you can extend the payment period. For example, extend a twenty-five-year mortgage to thirty years to reduce payments. If your mortgage is higher than prevailing rates, refinance at a lower rate. If you are a renter, consider moving to a unit that has lower rent than what you now pay.

• Utilities. You can reduce phone bills by making fewer long-distance calls. If it's necessary for you to make long-distance calls, sign up for a special rate reduction program sponsored by most long-distance carriers. Make calls during the hours when rates are lower. When you use the air conditioner and furnace, set the thermostat a little lower. Replace hundred-watt bulbs with sixty-watt bulbs. Turn off lights when rooms are not being used.

• Food. At the supermarket, buy store-brand foods that cost less. Buy your groceries at discount food warehouses where prices are usually lower than at supermarkets. Save and use food discount coupons.

• Medical. If you have to pay part or all of your health and accident insurance, shop for a plan that has the same benefits at less cost.

• Insurance. If you are like many people, you could have too much life insurance. For most young families, term insurance that is less costly than ordinary or whole life insurance may be adequate. Compare auto and housing insurance rates from more than one company for the same coverage at less cost.

Reducing Discretionary Cost Items

Now look at your discretionary items in column B of the worksheet. This is where you can reduce many costs. Some things to consider are these.

• Clothing. Ask yourself if you can buy less expensive clothes and still look well groomed. Could you get by with fewer new clothes?

• Personal care. Make fewer trips to the beauty salon or barber shop to cut expenses. With today's new fabrics and spot removers, you can reduce dry cleaning costs.

• Newspapers, books, and magazines. Is all the reading material you buy necessary? Do you read all the publications to which you subscribe? Use the library more often. A good library carries most of the better publications.

• Transportation. Could you car pool, take the bus, or ride the subway to and from work to cut expenses? Public transportation is usually less expensive than driving your auto.

• Education. Choose a public over a private school for your children's education. Instead of paying for an expensive course at night school, buy a book that covers the material, and study at home. Buy school supplies and clothes off-season at discount stores.

• Travel. Long vacation trips can be expensive. Instead of a two-week vacation away from home, limit your time away to one week. Spend the second week on short, less costly trips close to home.

• Entertainment. Host fewer parties during the year and serve roast beef instead of steak. Occasionally serve wine at parties instead of more expensive liquor. Go less frequently to plays, movies, costly restaurants, and social affairs to reduce expenses.

• Gifts. Buy less costly gifts for anniversaries, weddings, and other special occasions.

• Other ways to cut expenses. Shop at discount stores, where prices are generally lower than at retail stores. Compare prices and products at several stores before you buy to get the best product at the lowest price. Limit the amount you spend playing the lottery. Instead of buying a new car every few years, drive the old one a year or two longer. Cancel your high-cost health club membership and exercise at home or in the park.

These are some of the ways to reduce living and discretionary cost items. Your aim should be to search for ways to cut your expenses, to free more money for investing.

One way to use the monthly income and expenses worksheet is to set aside a specific amount each month for investing after living expenses are paid. Then apportion the remainder of your monthly income among your discretionary items. This is called paying yourself first—before you spend money for nonessential items.

CREDIT CARD REVIEW

As many people know, there are several ways to get into debt. Most people use mortgage debt when they buy a house, and borrow to finance the purchase of an automobile. These are useful ways to purchase essential living needs.

The trouble with debt is that it can get out of control and become a problem before many borrowers even realize it. Probably the easiest way for debt to become a problem is with the excessive use of credit cards. Credit card interest rates generally range from 12 percent to 21 percent. If you must borrow money on a credit card, get one that charges a low interest rate. The rates on some cards are around 12 to 13 percent. What's more, if your credit card charges a high annual fee, switch to one with a low fee. Consider any amount over $25 a year as high.

It shouldn't be difficult to see how credit cards could place a burden on your finances. The burden results from the large amount of money you can borrow and the high interest charged by the lender. If you want to avoid financial trouble, then control the use of your credit cards.

Fortunately, you can determine if your use of credit cards is getting out of control by completing the credit card worksheet below. It will only take a few minutes, and it could be well worth the time spent. For simplicity, you should combine your credit debt on the worksheet.

CREDIT CARD WORKSHEET

	TYPE of CARD	TOTAL AMOUNT BORROWED	INTEREST RATE	OUT-STANDING BALANCE	MONTHLY PAYMENTS
1.	_____	_____	_____	_____	_____
2.	_____	_____	_____	_____	_____
3.	_____	_____	_____	_____	_____
4.	_____	_____	_____	_____	_____
5.	_____	_____	_____	_____	_____
Totals	_____	_____	_____	_____	_____

Appraisal:

(A) Monthly net income $ _____

(B) Total monthly credit card payments $ _____

(C) B divided by A = _____ percent of net income used to pay credit card debt

If C is greater than 20 percent, credit card debt may be out of control.

Reviewing the Credit Card Worksheet

Let's look at the credit card worksheet. Compare your total credit card payments on this worksheet and on the monthly income and expenses worksheet. The amounts should be the same. Credit debt is on the credit card worksheet so you know what percent of your monthly income goes for credit, and on the income and expenses worksheet as a discretionary item, which means you can do something about reducing it.

On the credit card worksheet, look at the interest rates you pay lenders for borrowing money. Are there any under

15 percent APR (annual percentage rate)? Compare the lender's rates with interest earned on a one-year certificate of deposit (CD) at a local bank. The difference between the two rates is probably 10 percent to 12 percent for the lender. It's no secret that the credit business is very profitable for the lender and a burden for the borrower.

Now total your outstanding card debt and divide it by the total of all your monthly credit card payments. The result is the number of months it will take to pay your outstanding debt, assuming there are no more charges.

If you use over 20 percent of your net income to pay for credit card debt, you could be headed for financial trouble, though individual cases vary. The 20 percent figure, of course, is only a guideline.

There's no doubt that credit card debt is a financial burden, unless the balance is paid within the card issuer's grace period. The uncontrolled use of these cards can push you deep into debt. Fortunately, you can do something to eliminate credit card debt.

Eliminating Credit Card Debt

The first action you can take to eliminate credit card debt is to limit the number of cards you own. Most people do not need to have more than three or four cards. One or two cards for business and travel expenses and one or two retail cards should be enough.

Next, if your outstanding card debt is at a high interest rate, try to pay it off with a bank or credit union loan at a lower rate. Thus, combine all your outstanding debt into a new loan at a lower interest ate.

Finally, assume no new credit card debt. When your current debt is paid off, pay any new bills within thirty days so no finance charges will accrue.

If you are going to build a good financial plan, one that will help you save a meaningful amount each month, you must exercise control over the use of your credit cards. Remember, it's difficult to invest objectively when you worry about debt.

UNDERSTANDING RISK

All investments carry a degree of risk—the chance that all or part of your money could be lost. Risk pertains not only to preserving the money that you invest but also to the return on your investments. This means that you can have relatively safe investments and still be susceptible to risk with respect to what your investments earn through interest, dividends, and capital gains.

When you invest, what are the risks? The major one is the risk that the after-tax return on your investments will not keep pace with the rate of inflation. For example, let's assume that you have a one-year CD that pays interest at 4 percent. If the rate of inflation is 4 percent and you are in the 28 percent tax bracket, the actual return on your CD is around minus 1 percent. If your CD is for $1,000, it would be worth only about $988 at the end of the year—certainly it is not a risk-free investment, since inflation consumes 4 percent and taxes 28 percent of your money. When you invest, inflation is the biggest and most certain risk you will face.

Another kind of risk is the possibility that your investments will drop below the price you paid for them. This is called market risk, and applies equally as well to gold, art, collectibles, and real estate as it does to stocks, bonds, and mutual funds.

You can largely offset market risk if you invest for the long term in good stocks and top-rated mutual funds. How is this possible? Historically, when the stock market has dropped, it eventually has risen above its earlier level, and the price of good stocks and the better funds have gone up with the market.

Since you cannot avoid risk when you invest, you need to find a way to manage risk. Before you make any investment decisions, determine the amount of risk you can accept. To help you determine this, the table below lists various investments by their level of risk and potential return. Review the investments and decide which ones you feel most comfortable with.

Relative Risk and Return Rankings

PLAN #1

Type of Investment	Risk Level	Potential Return
Government securities	Low	Medium
Municipal bonds	Low	Medium
Bank instruments	Medium	Low
Annuities	Medium	Low
Money market mutual funds	Medium	Medium
Corporate bonds	Medium	Medium
Bond mutual funds	Medium	Medium
Growth mutual funds	Medium	High
Quality growth stocks	Medium/High	High
Zero-coupon bonds	Medium/High	High
Rental real estate	High	Medium
Oil and gas limited partnerships	High	Medium
Numismatic coins	High	Low
Commodity contracts	High	High
Futures contracts	High	High

The risk level and potential return assigned to the investments in the table may vary according to who does the ranking, but there is general consensus on the investments that rank at the top and bottom of the table.

The amount of risk you can handle may depend on your income and family circumstances. For example, someone with high income and no dependents usually can handle more risk than someone with relatively low income and several dependents.

Don't let risk be the only factor when you make investment decisions. Weigh the risk of an investment against its return and then consider only investments that are within your comfort level.

EMERGENCY FUND

Before you invest, set up a fund for small and unexpected emergencies: The car always needs some repairs or the house requires a few improvements when you least expect it. The most obvious reason for an emergency fund is to pay for those small and unexpected expenses. Another reason is to have money available so you won't have to sell your investments for minor emergencies.

How much should you set aside in an emergency fund? The answer varies from family to family, but about three months of your net pay is the minimum amount. Today, with severance pay, unemployment insurance, company health benefits, and a growing job market, a three-month fund should be enough to cover any minor emergency.

In case of a major emergency, such as the loss of a job, disabling illness, or the death of a spouse, a three-month fund probably wouldn't cover all your expenses. It's the little crises, not the big ones, for which an emergency fund provides. If a major emergency occurs, the last resource to consider is your emergency fund. Better sources to pay for a major emergency are any dividends that you have accumulated in life insurance policies, borrowing against your company pension plan, and a home equity loan.

One way to save money for an emergency is to make periodic payments in a money market mutual fund (MMMF). In many ways, MMMFs are like checking accounts but better, since they usually pay a higher interest rate. Most MMMFs provide free checks for use against your deposits, but the minimum amount you can write is usually $500. A high minimum on checks is good since it could stop you from writing them for small, nonessential items.

Another way to save for an emergency is to have your bank take a deduction from your paycheck and deposit it in a negotiable order of withdrawal (NOW) account. Today most NOW accounts pay anywhere from 3 percent to 4 percent on the average monthly balance, but there is a service charge if the balance falls below the bank's minimum requirements.

One problem with an emergency fund is that it provides you with an opportunity to call any setback an emergency and spend the money. Therefore, you'll have to distinguish between a real emergency and what is merely a cost of living expense. Setting aside money for an emergency and using it only for a bona fide emergency is an essential part of any investment plan. And an emergency fund could be the difference between a good plan and one that is only ordinary.

COMPUTER-AIDED PLANNING

If you have a personal computer, it can help with your financial planning. All you need is the appropriate software package that will run on your computer.

Software packages vary by product, but many will balance checkbooks, create budgets, plan for taxes, track investments, and list expenses. Many packages have expense groupings for mortgage payments, groceries, insurance, utilities, and entertainment.

If you buy computer software to track your budget, be sure that the package provides names for different expense groupings, such as housing, food, utilities, and medical. And, that you can transfer information from one month to the next in case you want to revise your financial plan. If you have outstanding loans to track, make certain you select software that adjusts your loan balance after a payment, computes interest paid, and adjusts the principal.

It should be easy to find an acceptable software package. Two packages to consider are DeskMate Home Organizer and Quicken.

Investment Choices

Let's imagine that you inherit $50,000 and decide to invest the whole amount. Before you rush out to invest your $50,000, match the amount of risk you can accept with the investments that are available.

Investing in gold bullion or numismatic coins, for example, is very risky. Besides, these investments do not pay interest or dividends. Also, the true value of fixed income investments such as CDs and bonds are eroded by inflation. So what should you do with your money?

Here's a list of several investments. Their advantages and disadvantages are pointed out so you can decide which are the right ones for you.

GOVERNMENT SECURITIES

The federal government offers various forms of debt securities. Many are exempt from state and local taxes but subject to federal taxes. They are probably the safest investments available and provide an array of yields and maturity dates. Here are some government securities to consider as an investment.

Treasury Bills, Notes, and Bonds

Treasury bills are auctioned each week and sell at a discount to their par value, which is $10,000. If you don't have $10,000, less the discount, forget about treasury bills. They are short-term investments that mature in thirteen, twenty-six, or fifty-two weeks.

Treasury notes sell in denominations as low as $1,000 for those that mature in two to ten years. Some other notes require a minimum of $5,000. The yield on treasury notes is comparable to the yield on treasury bills.

Treasury bonds are longer-term investments that sell in denominations of $1,000 or more. Treasury bonds usually mature in five to thirty years, and some can be called in (redeemed) before their maturity date.

Federal Agency Securities

Securities are offered in $1,000 units or more by government agencies such as the Government National Mortgage Association, Federal National Mortgage Association, Student Loan Marketing Association, Federal Land Banks, and other federal agencies. They provide a greater yield to maturity than treasury securities, often a percentage point or so more. However, federal agency securities, unlike treasury securities, have no government guarantee for the payment of interest and return of principal, so they carry more risk. Because the price of agency securities fluctuates in relation to interest rates in general, their value goes down if new issues pay more than existing ones.

Series EE Savings Bonds

Series EE bonds, which originally were named Series E savings bonds, come in denominations of $50 to $10,000. There is no sales charge when you purchase or redeem Series EE bonds, and there is a 4 percent interest rate guarantee if you hold them for at least five years. You can defer the tax on their interest until the bonds mature or you redeem them. Since Series EE bonds are a safe investment with an average yield, they might fit your investment plan.

Government securities do have some good investment features. They are exempt from state and local taxes; you can replace them if they are lost; and, except for agency securities, they are backed by the federal government.

The disadvantages of investing in government securities are that most have a fixed rate of return that is usually lower than that of other types of investments; there is a maturity date that makes them somewhat illiquid; they are sold in denominations that may not fit everyone's budget; their price fluctuates as interest rates in general rise or fall; and their interest is not (except for Series EE bonds) reinvested or compounded.

One type of government security that you should avoid is the mortgage-backed security that contains a pool of mortgages. These securities come in packages called tranches. The problem with tranches is that their structure is so complex that it's difficult to determine exactly what you are buying or the risk level. Another problem is that the mortgages in the tranches can be refinanced, and you may receive a lower rate of return than you expect.

BANK INSTRUMENTS

Bank instruments include investments such as CDs, passbook savings accounts, NOW accounts, money market deposit accounts, and interest-paying checking accounts.

Bank instruments offer certain advantages. The first is safety. Your deposits are fully insured by the Federal Deposit Insurance Corporation up to $100,000, if the bank is covered by that organization. Second, bank accounts are easy to open and close and there are no sales commissions for deposits or withdrawals.

The disadvantages to bank instruments include penalties for early withdrawals on time deposits; being locked into a low-paying CD when interest rates rise; the requirement of a minimum balance to receive interest on checking; and a low rate of return compared to similar types of investments. For people who want a higher return on their money with slightly more risk, there are better investments available than what banks have to offer.

ANNUITIES

Annuities are sold primarily by life insurance companies and include two general types: single premium, which requires a large, one-time sum of money, and deferred, which requires monthly, quarterly, or yearly payments.

The main advantage to annuities is tax-deferment. Their disadvantages include high sales commissions, early withdrawal penalties, low rates of return, and poor management. Annuities are discussed in more detail in Chapter 9.

GOLD AND SILVER INVESTMENTS

Investing in gold and silver bullion or coins is very risky. At times, these investments can be a hedge against inflation, but other investments also do that.

Gold and silver bullion is bought and sold in relation to the price of the metals in the world markets. These prices can have wide fluctuations and have been going down for the past few years.

Gold and silver numismatic (rare) coins are bought and sold for their intrinsic value and the public's demand for them. The main drawback to numismatic coins is overgrading. For example, when a dealer sells a rare coin, it might be graded MS (Mint State)–65. However, when the purchaser sells the same coin, far too many times it is downgraded to less than MS–65. This results in a big loss to the person who sells the coin.

Coin dealers may cite a survey that rare coins were the best investment during a certain period. Often, however, these surveys are skewed by selecting only those coins that have appreciated the most. Most rare coins appreciate much less, and many even depreciate in value. Gold and silver investments are much too risky for the prudent investor.

LIMITED PARTNERSHIPS

Limited partnerships are like open-end mutual funds in that several people pool their money for investment purposes. While mutual funds invest primarily in stocks and bonds, limited partnerships may involve art, equipment leasing, real estate, oil and gas, and other types of investments.

In the 1980s, limited partnerships were popular as tax shelters and income-producing investments. Now that the tax laws have changed, limited partnerships have less appeal. Some weaker partnerships are being combined into new ones called master partnerships, but even these are not appealing.

The advantages of limited partnerships are that any loss is limited to your investment (if this can be called an advantage), and any earnings are usually paid directly to you without being taxed at the corporate level.

The drawbacks to limited partnerships include the problem of evaluating their worth as good investments, high commission charges, and difficulty in reselling them. Limited partnerships are risky and unattractive investments.

RENTAL REAL ESTATE

Today, rental real estate is no longer the "can't lose" investment that it was for so many years. The Tax Reform Act of 1986 ended most of the tax advantages of owning real estate other than your home.

The benefits of rental real estate are the possibility that it could increase in value and the leverage in financing it. However, at times, properties can be difficult to sell at the asking price. In addition, the maintenance and repair of rental properties may cause you irritation, considerable expense, and a major outlay of your time. There are better places than rental real estate to invest.

CORPORATE BONDS

Most corporate bonds are sold as unsecured debentures backed by the corporation that issued the bonds. They are usually issued in denominations of $1,000 and their market price is listed daily in most large newspapers. Since the interest paid by bonds is fixed, their price will fluctuate reflecting prevailing interest rates.

The main advantages of corporate bonds are that they pay a higher interest rate than government bonds and they are sold in denominations as low as $1,000.

Their disadvantages are that they may be redeemed by the issuer before they mature and the bondholder will no longer receive interest on the bonds; they fluctuate in price and if they are sold before maturity the bondholder could receive less than the price paid for them; corporations may default by not paying the principal and interest on their bonds; and they are not backed by the federal government.

MUNICIPAL BONDS

Municipal bonds, or tax-exempt bonds as they are often called, are issued by state and local governments. Most are general obligation bonds, with interest paid by the taxing power of the issuer, or revenue bonds, with interest paid from a specific project such as a toll bridge or road.

Whether the tax-exempt feature of a municipal bond is more favorable than a taxable bond depends on your income tax bracket and the yield of the bond. To determine whether a taxable or nontaxable bond provides the higher yield, determine your tax bracket and subtract it from one hundred, and divide the tax-exempt yield by the result. The percentage is equal to a taxable yield. For example, if you are in the 28 percent tax bracket, a 5 percent tax-exempt yield is equal to a 6.94 percent taxable yield.

The main advantage of municipal bonds is their tax-free status. Their disadvantages are that many lack marketability because they are issued by small communities and thus are not actively traded; there is a lack of information on them to determine their risk; and they usually come in denominations of $25,000 and up.

ZERO-COUPON BONDS

Zero-coupon bonds are debt securities that are issued at a discount from their face value. For example, you might pay

$100 for a $1,000 bond that yields 12 percent and matures in twenty years. The interest on zero-coupons is compounded and paid in a lump sum when they mature. Even though interest is not paid until maturity, the Internal Revenue Service requires that the owners of zero-coupons pay taxes on the interest earned each year as if it were actually received.

The advantages of investing in zero-coupons are that a relatively high rate of interest is earned if they are held to maturity, and they can be readily traded in the secondary bond market.

The drawbacks to zero-coupons are that they can be subject to wide price fluctuations; their yield is set at a fixed rate until maturity, which could be unfavorable to the bondholder should interest rates rise; they can be called in by the issuer before maturity; and there is always the chance of default.

BOND MUTUAL FUNDS

If you plan to buy government securities or corporate, municipal, and zero-coupon bonds, consider a no-load bond fund. Despite their tendency to change in price as interest rates fluctuate, bond funds appeal to many investors as a medium-risk, income-type of investment.

An investor in a bond fund essentially holds IOUs or promissory notes that pay interest at a fixed rate. In contrast, an investor in a stock fund is the part owner of a company and shares in possible earnings growth and the payment of dividends.

You'll find that a bond fund is less risky than owning an individual bond because a fund holds many bonds and, should one default, the remaining bonds would probably be secure. If you own an individual bond and it defaults, you could lose all of your investment.

If you invest in a bond fund, here are some points to consider:

- Bonds fluctuate in price as interest rates rise or fall, and you may have an emergency situation that requires you to sell your fund when its price is at its lowest.

- Generally, bond funds don't provide as high a total return as growth funds or common stocks.
- The fixed rate of return on a bond fund is a drawback in times of rapid inflation.
- Check several bond funds for one that charges a low rate for investing your money.
- Select a fund that holds at least BBB+ bonds as rated by Standard and Poor's. The higher the rating, the more secure the bonds. For example, AAA bonds are more secure than BBB+ bonds.
- Avoid bond funds with mortgage-backed securities.

COMMON STOCKS

Many people feel that investing in common stocks is too risky. To them, a passbook savings account, a CD, or a money market deposit account provides greater stability. It's true that the price of many stocks can be volatile at times, but it's also true that when you invest in quality stocks, you could be greatly rewarded.

Determining which are the quality stocks is not a time-consuming or difficult process. It involves developing some stock selection criteria and disciplining yourself to stick with them. With selecting criteria, you increase your chance of buying quality stocks. If you invest in stocks, Chapter 7 provides some helpful investment guidelines.

There are two good reasons for buying stocks: They provide capital gains should their price go up, and many pay dividends. What's more, many of the stocks that pay dividends have a dividend reinvestment program (DRP). In this program, you can reinvest all or a portion of the dividends you receive to purchase additional shares of a company's stock, usually at a reduced market price and no commission. Of course, dividends that are reinvested can be withdrawn at any time.

Not everyone should invest in stocks. The volatility of the stock market can be too stressful for some people. However, if you can handle the fluctuations of the market, you can include stocks in your investment plan.

MONEY MARKET MUTUAL FUNDS

No matter what your experience in financial matters, there is always a need to have some assets that you can quickly convert to cash. A money market mutual fund can fill that need.

Money market mutual funds can be taxable or tax-free. The taxable funds invest in short-term money market instruments such as commercial paper, CDs, and banker's acceptances (used to finance international commercial transactions), while the tax-free funds invest primarily in the short-term maturing bonds of states and municipalities.

MMMFs are especially attractive because of the services they provide to their shareholders. These services include reinvestment of dividends, check-writing privileges, record-keeping, and the opportunity to transfer money from one fund to another.

Although they are not insured, MMMFs are one of the safest investments available, and not one has failed. They are liquid, which means you can easily convert shares into cash with the use of a check-writing privilege. Also, they pay a relatively high yield that varies with interest rates in general. What's more, because most of the securities held by MMMFs are of large denominations, the small investor receives the same yield as the large investor.

Since the price per share of MMMFs is held constant at $1, a shareholder cannot receive less than his or her original investment. In contrast, the share price of other types of mutual funds rises and falls as the securities held in the fund change in value.

Because of their safety, convenience, and relatively high yield, MMMFs are good investments for most people. In addition, they can serve as an emergency fund and a temporary place to hold money for investing elsewhere.

GROWTH MUTUAL FUNDS

Growth funds appeal to many investors in mutual funds. Growth funds invest primarily in the common stock of companies that are expected to increase in market value at an accelerated rate. Such funds put more importance on capital gains and less on current income or yield. The price of growth funds is apt to be more volatile than that of most other funds, but they have the potential to provide a much greater return. Many growth funds are good long-term investments for capital appreciation and some dividend income.

Because of the many desirable features of growth funds, it's a good idea to consider one as the main holding in your investment plan. Later on, as you gain experience and confidence, you can diversify with common stocks, bond funds, and other types of investments.

SUMMING UP

The list of investment choices does not include every way your money can be put to work. It covers only those investments that are readily available and those with adequate information about their past performance.

It's to your advantage to stick with sound and secure investments such as money market funds, growth funds, bond funds, top-rated zero-coupon bonds, Series EE bonds, and quality common stocks. These investments are easy to buy and sell, and information on them is always available.

It's usually best to avoid investments such as gold and silver, limited partnerships, rental real estate, and bank instruments, such as CDs, whose true value is eroded by inflation.

When you invest, the preservation of your capital should be your main concern. To preserve your capital, keep away from investments that carry a lot of risk and those that can't keep up with inflation, and you should come out ahead.

3

Basis of Mutual Funds

There are two general types of mutual funds: closed-end and open-end. Closed-end funds have a fixed number of shares and usually trade on one of the stock exchanges. Open-end funds, the more popular of the two types, have an unlimited number of shares and are not listed on an exchange. This book covers only open-end funds, since they usually provide shareholders a greater investment return than closed-end funds.

An open-end mutual fund is a company that pools money from shareholders and invests it in securities such as stock, bonds, and cash equivalents. The number of securities in a fund may range from as few as twenty-five to fifty, to as many as a few hundred. When you buy shares in an open-end fund, you own a portion of the securities held in the fund. As the securities move up and down, the price of your fund changes accordingly.

TYPES OF OPEN-END
MUTUAL FUNDS

Since there are so many open-end mutual funds, it is difficult to classify them by type or investment objective. For example, a fund with an objective to invest in small growth companies may also hold shares in medium-sized growth companies. Another fund's objective may be to provide its shareholders with maximum dividend income but hold shares in companies that pay relatively low dividends. Probably the best classifications of open-end mutual funds are the ones issued by the Investment Company Institute in its *Directory of Mutual Funds*:

Aggressive growth funds "seek maximum capital gains as their investment objective. Current income is not a significant factor. Some may invest in stocks of businesses that are somewhat out of the mainstream, such as fledgling companies, new industries, companies fallen on hard times, or industries temporarily out of favor. Some may also use specialized investment techniques such as option writing or short-term trading."

Balanced funds "generally have a three-part investment objective: to conserve the investors' initial principal, to pay current income, and to promote a long-term growth of both this principal and income."

Corporate bond funds, "like income funds, seek a high level of income. They do so by buying bonds of corporations for the majority of the fund's portfolio. The rest of the portfolio may be in U.S. Treasury bonds or bonds issued by a federal agency."

Flexible portfolio funds "may be 100 percent invested in stocks or bonds or money market instruments, depending on market conditions. These funds give the money managers the greatest flexibility in anticipating or responding to economic changes."

GNMA or Ginnie Mae funds "invest in mortgage securities backed by the Government National Mortgage Association (GNMA). To qualify for this category, the majority of the portfolio must always be invested in mortgage-backed securities."

Global bond funds "invest in the debt securities of companies and countries worldwide, including the U.S."

Global equity funds "invest in securities traded worldwide, including the U.S. Compared to direct investments, global funds offer investors an easy avenue to investing abroad. The funds' professional money managers handle the trading and recordkeeping details and deal with differences in currencies, languages, time zones, laws and regulations, and business customs and practices. In addition to another layer of diversification, global funds add another layer of risk—exchange-rate risk."

Growth funds "invest in the common stock of well-established companies. Their primary aim is to produce an increase in the value of their investments (capital gains) rather than a flow of dividends. Investors who buy a growth fund are more interested in seeing the fund's share price rise than receiving income from dividends."

Growth and income funds "invest mainly in the common stock of companies that have had increasing share value but also a solid record of paying dividends. This type of fund attempts to combine long-term capital growth with a steady stream of income."

High-yielding bond funds "maintain at least two-thirds of their portfolios in lower rated corporate bonds (Baa or lower by Moody's rating service and BBB or lower by Standard and Poor's rating service). In return for a generally higher yield, investors must bear a greater degree of risk than for higher-rated bonds."

Income (bond) funds "seek a high level of current income for their shareholders by investing at all times in a mix of corporate and government bonds."

Income (equity) funds "seek a high level of current income for their shareholders by investing primarily in equity securities of companies with good dividend-paying records."

Income (mixed) funds "seek a high level of current income for their shareholders by investing in income-producing securities, including both equity and debt instruments."

International funds "invest in equity securities of companies located outside the U.S. Two-thirds of their portfolios must be so invested at all times to be categorized here."

Long-term municipal bond funds "invest in bonds issued by states and municipalities to finance schools, highways, hospitals, airports, bridges, water and sewer works, and other public projects. In most cases, income earned on these securities is not taxed by the federal government, but may be taxed under state and local laws. For some taxpayers, portions of income earned on these securities may be subject to the federal alternative minimum tax."

Money market mutual funds "invest in the short-term securities sold in the money market. These are generally the safest, most stable securities available, including treasury bills, certificates of deposit of large banks, and commercial paper (the short-term IOUs of large U.S. corporations)."

Precious metals/gold funds "maintain two-thirds of their portfolios invested in securities associated with gold, silver, and other precious metals."

Short-term municipal bond funds "invest in municipal securities with relatively short maturities. These are also known as tax-exempt money market funds. For some taxpayers portions of income from these securities may be subject to the federal alternative minimum tax."

Long-term state municipal bond funds "work just like other long-term municipal bond funds (see above) except their portfolios contain the issues of only one state. A resident of that state has the advantage of receiving income free of both federal and state tax. For some taxpayers, portions of income from these securities may be subject to the federal alternative minimum tax."

Short-term state municipal bond funds "work just like other short-term municipal bond funds (see above) except their portfolios contain the issues of only one state. A resident of that state has the advantage of receiving income free of both federal and state tax. For some taxpayers, portions of income from these securities may be subject to the federal alternative minimum tax."

U.S. government income funds "invest in a variety of government securities. These include U.S. Treasury bonds, federally guaranteed mortgage-backed securities, and other government notes."

Additional Information

You can request a copy of the *Directory of Mutual Funds* from the Investment Company Institute, 1401 H Street NW, Washington, DC 20005, telephone number 202-326-5800.

This publication, which costs $8.50, contains helpful information about investing in mutual funds.

PROSPECTUS

A mutual fund cannot sell you shares without giving you a prospectus, the official document that describes a fund and its policies. A prospectus should provide enough information so you can decide if you want to invest in a fund. It's a good idea to check more than one prospectus so you will select a fund that meets your investment objectives. Here's a rundown on the most important items to check in a prospectus.

Objective

In the prospectus, all funds specify their investment objective. For example, an objective could be long-term growth of capital, high level of current income, or some other investment goal. The objective can range from low-risk and high-return investments to high-risk and low-return investments. Make certain that the fund's objective is compatible with your reasons for investing in it.

Annual Operating Expenses

Annual operating expenses usually consist of two charges: management fees and other expenses. The operating expenses of most funds are between 0.75 percent and 1.75 percent of net assets. In addition to operating expenses, there are sales charges, such as front-end loads or back-end loads. These charges are described in Chapter 5.

Other Information

A prospectus usually includes this additional information:

- The fund's performance since it began operations.
- How to purchase shares.
- How to redeem shares.
- Minimum investment required.
- The fund's management.

- Dividend and capital gains distributions.
- Portfolio turnover.
- Dividend reinvestment plan.
- Automatic monthly investment plan.
- Shareholder rights.
- How to convert to another fund.
- Check-writing privileges.
- Income tax advice.
- Special services, such as telephone exchange of shares.

MANAGEMENT OF FUNDS

Although a mutual fund is essentially owned by its shareholders, a board of directors is responsible for administering the fund's investment policy, including the selection of the fund manager. The manager is usually paid a fee based on the fund's total assets to handle the securities in the fund. A transfer agent, usually a bank, maintains records for the fund's shareholders.

NET ASSET VALUE

The net asset value (NAV) is the price of a fund's shares. The NAV is calculated each business day by subtracting liabilities from the value of securities held in the fund and dividing by the number of shares outstanding.

INITIAL INVESTMENT MINIMUM

The minimum initial investment to open an account is set by each fund. A few funds have no minimum, and others require as much as several hundred dollars. However, most set their minimum between $500 and $1,000. The minimum for later investments is much lower than the initial investment minimum, usually from $50 to $100. The minimum to open an individual retirement account (IRA) is usually less than the minimum for a regular investment, on average about $250.

DISTRIBUTIONS

When you buy shares in a mutual fund, you must decide whether to reinvest any dividends and capital gains distributions paid by the fund. Most shareholders reinvest their distributions to buy additional shares in the fund, rather than receiving them in cash.

Since mutual funds register with the Securities and Exchange Commission (SEC) as regulated investment companies, they do not pay taxes if they distribute their investment dividends and most capital gains to their shareholders. They merely serve as conduits for distributions to pass from the fund to their shareholders. Except for some municipal bond funds, all distributions you receive are taxable, and you must report them to the IRS.

LEGISLATION

Federal and state laws regulate the activities of mutual funds. These laws require the disclosure of fund operations to the SEC, state regulators, and their shareholders. Four federal laws regulate mutual funds.

• Securities Act of 1933. This law requires that all mutual funds file a registration statement and provide information to the SEC. It also directs funds to provide current and potential investors with a prospectus that contains information on the fund's management, objectives, and policy.

• Securities Exchange Act of 1934. This act makes funds liable to antifraud provisions and regulation by the SEC and the National Association of Securities Dealers.

• Investment Advisors Act of 1940. This legislation regulates the actions of investment advisers to mutual funds.

• Investment Company Act of 1940. This act contains provisions to prevent conflicts of interest and self-dealing in the management of funds.

RECORDKEEPING AND REPORTING

Most mutual funds maintain good records for their share-holders. Each time you make an investment, redeem shares, or receive a distribution, you receive a confirmation that contains the following:

- Date of the transaction.
- Dollar amount of the transaction.
- Price at which shares were bought and sold.
- Number of shares bought or sold.
- Total shares held in your account.

You'll also get quarterly or semiannual reports as well as a yearly report from your fund. These reports show the securities held by the fund, the fund's performance during the reporting period, and other financial information.

At the end of each year, you will receive a Form 1099-DIV that shows all distributions paid to you by the fund. The 1099 form separates dividends and capital gains distributions. This division is useful since you can offset capital gains against capital losses for tax purposes.

4

Mutual Funds— Advantages and Disadvantages

Mutual funds offer something for all kinds of investors. Some investors buy them for their security; others for their services. Many find them attractive to save for the down payment on a house, for college expenses for the children, or for supplementing retirement.

There are three ways to make money in mutual funds: through dividends and interest earned by a fund's securities; when the securities held by a fund are sold at a profit; and through any increase in the value of the securities held by a fund.

There is no guarantee that a fund will provide you with a generous return. Yet the return on many funds has been very good. Usually, the longer your investment period, the greater your return.

Keep in mind that there are disadvantages to mutual funds, but they are surpassed by the advantages that funds offer. Let's look at their advantages.

ADVANTAGES OF MUTUAL FUNDS

Professional Management

Mutual fund managers are full-time, experienced professionals. Most of them have a good investment strategy that many individual investors may lack. For this reason, many managers attract investors to their particular funds.

Since they have a large amount of money to invest, fund managers can get the latest information about securities, which may be difficult for the small investor to obtain. Managers usually base their investment decisions on factors such as the growth potential of particular industries, earnings outlook for individual securities, and general economic conditions. Few individual investors can match the experience and skill of fund managers.

Diversification

Diversification is an investment principle that requires holding more than one type of security to reduce risk. To diversify their portfolios, mutual fund managers invest in securities such as common stocks, bonds, and money market funds.

When you invest in a fund, you automatically own a portion of several securities, a diversified portfolio. When the price of a fund goes down, some of its securities may drop substantially in price, while others may drop only slightly or even increase in price.

One type of fund is not highly diversified. This is the specialty or sector fund, which invests in a specific industry such as utilities, energy, health care, or technology. However, this type still diversifies within the specific industry.

There is also an unfavorable side to diversification. A fund may invest in so many different securities that its performance only matches the market indexes. All types of securities move in cycles, and the ideal approach is for a fund to catch the right one on the upswing, whether it is a group of stocks or an industry. What works best is the right diversification at a particular time.

Regulation

Federal and state laws tightly regulate what mutual funds can and cannot do with their investors' money. These laws require that funds disclose their operations to the SEC and other regulatory authorities. In addition, funds must furnish their shareholders with periodic statements that disclose their current securities and latest investment results.

Conveniences

It's easy and convenient to invest in a fund. You can handle the paperwork to open an account and make later investments from your home. The fund takes care of the bookkeeping and provides you with an account statement after each of your investments.

To open an account, all you do is telephone the investment company that handles the fund and ask for a prospectus, which is free of charge. Then, if the prospectus meets your investment requirements, complete the application and return it to the fund. Most funds maintain toll-free telephone lines in case you have any questions about the prospectus.

Low Initial Investment

Some funds require no minimum initial investment. However, many do have a minimum that is usually within the budget of most investors. The relatively low minimum proves helpful to people who have a limited amount to invest at one time.

Shareholder Services

Mutual funds provide many services to their shareholders, and they continue to provide more and better services each year. Funds provide many services including the following:

• Voluntary savings. No-load funds are voluntary as opposed to contractual load funds that charge a commission and may require periodic investments. In a no-load fund, you can make your initial investment and purchase additional shares at any time without charge.

- Automatic monthly investment plan. Once you open an account with a fund, you may authorize your bank to make regular payments from your checking or savings account to the fund. Most banks will honor automatic transfer of funds, but you should check with your bank first to ensure that it has this service. In addition, your employer may have a payroll deduction plan that will automatically deduct money from your salary and send it to your fund.

- Automatic reinvestment of distributions. If you choose, you can reinvest all or part of the dividends and capital gains distributions paid by a fund to buy additional shares. This is done through a fund's automatic reinvestment plan (ARP). An ARP is a good idea not only because it gives you the opportunity to acquire more shares but also because it prevents you from spending the distributions if you receive them in cash. There is no minimum investment requirement when you reinvest your distributions.

The reinvestment of distributions is a means of forced savings that incorporates the principle of dollar-cost averaging, a method of investing at regular intervals. The idea is that you will purchase more shares when the price of a fund is low and fewer shares when it is high.

- Conversion privileges. Many funds are part of a family of funds that usually includes stock, bond, and money market funds. Some families even include international, specialty, sector, and commodity funds. If your fund is part of a family, you usually can switch from one fund to another within the family. Since your investment goals may change through the years, the privilege to switch funds is an important service. For tax purposes, the exchange of one fund for another is treated as a sale and must be reported to the IRS for the year the exchange is made.

- Systematic withdrawal plans. Many funds have a withdrawal plan that will allow you to receive payments at regular intervals. You can receive payments from dividends, capital gains, or the principal in your fund on a monthly or quarterly basis. However, most funds require a minimum balance of $5,000 to participate in the plan.

• Liquidity. You can cash in all or part of your shares in a fund at any time and receive their current market value, which may be greater or less than your original cost. Most funds will redeem shares upon a written request. However, when the redemption exceeds a specific amount, many funds require a signature guarantee.

• Recordkeeping. Most mutual funds keep good records for their shareholders. When you make an investment, redeem shares, or switch from one fund to another, you will receive a confirmation of the transaction from the fund. Depending on the fund's policy, you will also receive an update of your account on a quarterly, semiannual or yearly basis.

• Ease of investing. Once you open an account, there are usually three convenient ways to invest in your fund. You may transfer money to your fund from your bank or your place of employment, invest by telephone or wire, or mail payments to your fund.

DISADVANTAGES OF MUTUAL FUNDS

Although mutual funds have a lot to offer, they still have their disadvantages, the biggest of which is the high cost of investing in funds. This is seen in funds that have front-end loads, 12b-1 fees, or back-end loads. In Chapter 5, you'll learn how to avoid these charges when you invest in pure no-load funds.

A fund's performance can be another drawback. Some funds consistently earn an above-average return; others perform poorly. The idea is to select a fund that, through the years, has consistently provided a good return.

A final criticism of mutual funds is the handling of capital gains. If you own a fund that pays capital gains, taxes must be paid on the gains for the year you receive them. If you own an individual stock, you pay no capital gains tax until the stock is sold.

5

Selecting a Mutual Fund

With so many mutual funds to choose from, you may wonder how to select one. It's not as difficult as it may seem. The first step is to take another look at your investment goals. Next, review the amount of investment risk you can handle. And then develop some criteria to select a fund.

MATCH YOUR INVESTMENT GOALS WITH YOUR RISK LEVEL

Before you select a fund, reexamine your investment goals. Your goals will help to determine the type of fund to invest in. For example, if you want to invest to supplement your retirement, which is over five years away, consider a growth fund. But if you are within five years of retirement and will need extra income, a growth and income fund may be best.

Next, review the investment risk that you feel comfortable with. Do you have a low-, medium-, or high-risk level when you invest? If you worry a lot about your investments, then you probably have a low-risk level. On the other hand, if you are the type of person who can handle the price fluctuations of the more volatile funds, you probably have a high-risk level.

If risk doesn't bother you, consider either an aggressive growth fund or a growth fund. If you can handle only a medium amount of risk, think about a growth and income fund. If you want to play it safe with low risk and moderate investment income, consider a U.S. government income fund.

After you decide your investment goals and your risk level, match them with a fund's objective. To do that, turn to Chapter 3 and select the type of fund with the objective that meets your requirements. The idea is to match your investment goals with the objective of a fund at the level of risk you feel comfortable with. Once you identify the type of fund that meets your investment requirements, set up selection criteria to screen the available funds.

SELECTION CRITERIA

Few people would buy a house without first looking at several and then selecting the one that best meets their needs. You should select a mutual fund the same way. Thus it's a good idea to set up selection criteria to help you screen the available funds. The most important criteria are performance, cost, and services. If a fund rates high on all three, consider it for your investment plan.

Performance

Before you buy shares in a mutual fund, you should review its past performance—its track record, the fund's rate of return compared to other funds and the market indexes. Although the past performance of a fund is not always an indication of its future investment results, it is still a good measure to use when you select a fund. It's better to consider only those funds that have been good performers for several years. You'll find that some funds perform well for a year or so, but have a poor overall record.

What is the best way to determine a fund's performance? You measure its performance against an index that is indicative of the stock market. Since stock market indexes assess the up and down price movements in their component stocks, you can use them as a yardstick for measuring a fund's performance. There are several market indexes, but the three most widely used are the Dow-Jones Industrial Average, Standard and Poor's 500 Index, and the NASDAQ (National Association of Security Dealers Automated Quotation System) Composite Index.

The Dow-Jones Industrial Average of thirty stocks, probably the best known of all the indexes, measures general stock market price movements. The Dow-Jones is called an average rather than an index because no adjustment is made in the number of shares outstanding in its component stocks.

Some complaints have been directed at the Dow-Jones. One is that it samples too small a percentage of the stocks listed on the New York Stock Exchange. Although the sample includes about 25 percent of the total value of all stocks on the exchange, it is still small. Another complaint is that the Dow-Jones contains too many cyclical stocks and under-represents growth stocks. Nevertheless, the Dow-Jones Industrial Average is the main index most people use when referring to the stock market.

The Standard and Poor's (S&P) 500 is the index most mutual fund managers use to measure their fund's performance. Within the S&P 500 are over four hundred industrial, forty utility, and twenty transportation stocks. This index includes stocks that represent over 75 percent of the market value of all those on the New York Stock Exchange.

The NASDAQ Composite Index is a computerized price reporting system that covers more than two thousand over-the-counter (OTC) stocks. This index includes industrial, bank, insurance, finance, transportation, and utility stocks.

If you measure a fund's performance against an index, be certain to use the appropriate one. For example, if a fund holds stocks that are listed on the New York and NASDAQ exchanges, use the S&P 500 to measure its performance. Use the NASDAQ Composite for a fund that invests primarily in OTC stocks, and the Dow-Jones averages when a fund invests mainly in stocks on the Dow-Jones. When you compare a fund's performance to a market index, be sure to consider the reinvestment of dividends and capital gains that the fund pays.

Cost

You can invest in a mutual fund without the use of a full-service broker, insurance agent, or financial adviser—who sell only front-end load funds. You can deal directly with a no-load fund and thus avoid all commissions.

To further reduce your expenses, you can invest in a fund that has no back-end load or 12b-1 fees. The following are all the fees that a fund can impose. It's a good idea to become familiar with these fees before you invest in a fund.

• Management and customer service fees. You pay fees to the investment company for the management and services that a fund provides. Since both load and no-load funds have the fees, they cannot be avoided. In a fund's prospectus, the fees are listed as a percentage of the fund's net assets and usually total 0.75 percent to 1.75 percent.

• Front-end load. Front-end load is a sales charge or commission ranging from 2.0 percent to 8.5 percent that a load fund deducts from each investment. For example, if your initial investment is $1,000 and the sales commission is 8.5 percent, your actual investment is only $915. What's more, the fund levies the commission on later investments and the reinvestment of distributions. Over several years, commissions amount to a lot of money—money that is deducted from your investment with no benefit to you.

• Back-end load. Some funds assess a charge when you redeem shares, called a back-end load. It can amount to 4 percent to 8 percent of the value of the redemption. Funds that don't have front-end loads often assess back-end loads as a way to hide their commissions.

• 12b-1 Fee. A 12b-1 fee is also known as a hidden load. The original intent of the fee was to aid funds with their marketing and distribution expenses. However, its original purpose may have changed to gouge the naive investor. The 12b-1 fee can amount to as much as 2 percent to 3 percent of what is deducted from your investments in a fund.

Here's an illustration of how fees can affect your investment in a fund. Let's take a hypothetical situation and assume that you make a lump-sum investment of $1,000 in an 8.5 percent load fund that has a 12b-1 fee of 1 percent, redemption fee of 5 percent, and service charge of 1 percent. We'll further assume that you sell the fund after one year with no change in its price.

Cost of your initial investment (8.5 percent of $1,000)	$85
Redemption charge (5 percent of $915)	$46
12b-1 fee (1 percent of $1,000)	$10
Management and customer service fee (1 percent of $1,000)	$10
Total charges	$151
Amount you receive at redemption	$849
Percent of loss on your investment	15.1%

An investment of $1,000 for one year in this hypothetical fund has charges of $151. Compare this to a pure no-load fund—a fund with no front-end load, back-end load, or 12b-1 fee—that charges only $10 for management and service fees. In addition, there is no clear evidence that load funds per se outperform no-load funds.

When you invest in a fund, there is no valid reason to pay a front-end load, back-end load, or 12b-1 fee. Read a fund's prospectus carefully, and if there are fees other than a management and customer service charge, reject it.

Services

The third selection item to consider is the services a fund offers its shareholders. If you follow the suggestions in this book, you will consider only no-load funds. You'll find that these funds provide convenient and reliable services to their shareholders, and there are no high-pressure sales tactics by their representatives.

No-load funds provide many services that you can access by mail or telephone. You can open an account with a fund and make periodic investments by mail. You can usually sell all or part of the shares you own in a fund by telephone.

Make certain before you open an account that a fund provides all the services that you want.

OTHER SELECTION CRITERIA

Besides performance, cost, and services, here are some other criteria to consider when you select a fund.

Management Changes

A fund's performance is closely tied to its management. Thus, it's a good idea to note any recent changes in the top management of a fund. A change in management does not mean that a fund will perform better or worse than before the change. What it does mean, however, is that new management may bring with it a new investment philosophy or strategy that is different from yours.

Business Week's yearly Mutual Fund Scoreboard covers whether current management has held the job for at least ten years. This publication as well as the fund itself will give you an indication about the tenure of a fund's management.

Risk

All investments, including mutual funds, involve risk. It's much easier to assess risk when you invest in gold, commodities, and limited partnerships than in various mutual funds.

Sometimes those funds that perform the best over the long term are the ones that are willing to take added risk by investing in more speculative stocks. Looking at the past performance of a fund, covering several years, is more important than trying to determine a fund's risk.

Some financial publications use betas to determine a fund's risk. A beta usually measures a fund's volatility to that of the S&P Index over a period of years. For example, if a fund's beta is 1.00 it should move with the S&P. A fund with a beta of 1.60 is 60 percent more volatile than the S&P Index and is presumably more risky.

Although betas provide some indication of risk, they should not be given too much weight when you consider a fund. As a rule, a fund's past performance is a more important selection factor than its beta.

Turnover Ratio

Turnover ratio is the yearly rate at which a fund buys and sells securities in its portfolio. A high turnover ratio is not evidence that a fund's performance will be good or poor. Often, a high turnover may indicate that the fund's manager is rotating investments into stock groups that show promise of increasing in value and out of those that are decreasing. In market advances, stock leadership changes from one industry group to another and fund managers may sell lagging groups and buy advancing ones. Other managers may sell those stocks whose balance sheets or price movement charts are turning negative and buy those which look more promising.

One effect of a high turnover rate is that fund expenses increase. These consist of brokerage commissions and the bid/ask price spreads for buying stocks. However, don't let a high turnover rate stop you from investing in a fund that meets your other selection criteria.

Size of Fund

With few exceptions, large funds are seldom the top performers in a rising market and seldom the worst performers in a falling market. What amount of assets makes a fund large? The figure is arbitrary, depending on whose yardstick you use. However, for our purposes, funds with assets over $500 million will be considered large.

The larger funds, because of their huge assets, usually invest in companies that have many shares outstanding. Thus, they may miss the opportunity to invest in smaller companies with fewer shares and greater growth potential. There is no doubt that smaller funds can be more flexible with their investment decisions since they can buy shares in relatively small companies that can be good performers in a rising market.

New Funds

Although it's best to base your selection of a fund on the performance, cost, and services of established funds, there may be times when you want to invest in a new fund. Since new funds have no investment record on which to judge their performance, it's usually better to avoid them.

However, there is an exception to investing in new funds. When an investment company that manages existing funds that are good performers offers a new fund, it presumably could perform as well as the existing funds that the investment company manages.

Buying Shares

There are four ways to buy shares in a mutual fund: through a brokerage house, insurance company, or financial adviser, or directly from the fund. When you buy a pure no-load fund, you deal directly with the fund and you pay no sales commission. Why pay a broker, an insurance agent, or financial adviser a 2 percent to 8.5 percent commission for something that you can do yourself?

To buy shares in a no-load fund, all that's required is that you call or write the fund for a free prospectus. If the prospectus meets your selection criteria, fill out the enclosed application and mail it to the fund with a check to cover your initial investment.

Since a prospectus is usually in legal-type language, it can be difficult to understand. If you have any questions, contact the fund and request a "statement of additional information" which has more details on the prospectus.

In addition to dealing directly with a fund, you can contact Charles Schwab & Company, a discount brokerage, which handles several no-load funds for a small fee.

PURE NO-LOAD FUNDS

The following list includes many pure no-load growth funds—funds that have no front-end load, back-end load, or 12b-1 fee. The list is a good starting point for the selection of a fund. For a free copy of a fund's prospectus, call the telephone number on the right side of the list.

Selected No-load Growth Funds
With No 12b-1 Fees or Back-end Loads

FUND	MINIMUM INITIAL INVESTMENT	FIVE-YEAR AVERAGE ANNUAL TOTAL RETURN (PERCENT)*	TELEPHONE NUMBERS 800		IN-STATE
AARP Capital Growth	$ 500	13.9	253-2277	MA	617-330-5400
Columbia Growth	$ 250	16.2	547-1707	OR	503-222-3606
Dreyfus Growth Opportunity	$2,500	9.7	645-6561	NY	718-895-1206
Dreyfus Third Century	$2,500	12.5	645-6561	NY	718-895-1206
Fidelity Ret. Growth	$2,500	18.2	544-8888	MA	617-439-0547
Fidelity Trend	$2,500	16.9	544-8888	MA	617-439-0547
Founders Special	$1,000	20.7	525-2440	CO	303-394-4404
Janus	$1,000	19.7	525-8983	CO	303-333-3863
Janus Twenty	$1,000	22.0	525-8983	CO	303-333-3863
Monetta	$ 100	16.2	666-3882	IL	708-462-9800

(continued)

Selected No-load Growth Funds
With No 12b-1 Fees or Back-end Loads *(continued)*

FUND	MINIMUM INITIAL INVESTMENT	FIVE-YEAR AVERAGE ANNUAL TOTAL RETURN (PERCENT)*	TELEPHONE NUMBERS 800		IN-STATE
Nicholas	$ 500	15.0	None	WI	414-272-6133
Northeast Inv. Growth	$1,000	13.4	225-6704	MA	617-523-3588
T. Rowe Price Amer.	$2,500	20.5	638-5660	MD	410-547-2308
Safeco Growth	$1,000	14.3	426-6730	WA	206-545-5530
Scudder Capital Growth	$1,000	15.3	225-2470	MA	617-439-4640
Sentry	$ 200	13.9	533-7827	WI	None
Steinroe Special	$1,000	19.0	338-2550	IL	312-368-7800
Steinroe Common Stock	$1,000	20.3	338-2550	IL	312-368-7800
20th Century Growth	None	18.2	345-2021	MO	816-531-5575
20th Century Select	None	14.9	345-2021	MO	816-531-5575
Value Line	$1,000	17.4	223-0818	NY	212-687-3965

* Note: includes change in net asset value and reinvestment of dividends and distributions for the period ending December 31, 1993.

FAMILY OF FUNDS

Many mutual funds are part of a larger grouping called a family of funds. The individual funds within the family have different portfolio managers but are under the direction of the same investment company. A family may include stock, bond, treasury, and money market funds. When you select a fund that belongs to a family, you can usually switch to another fund within the family. The opportunity to switch funds is useful since your investment objectives may change through the years. In addition, you could maintain a money market fund for emergency purposes within the family.

Here's a table of pure no-load fund families that have growth as well as money market mutual funds. You can obtain a prospectus on any of these funds by calling the number in the table.

No-Load Families
With Growth and Money Market Funds

| | TELEPHONE | | |
| | TOLL FREE | | |
FUND FAMILY	1-800	IN-STATE	HOME STATE
Bull and Bear	847-4200	212-363-1100	New York
Columbia	547-1707	503-222-3606	Oregon
Evergreen	235-0064	914-694-2020	New York
Fidelity	544-8888	617-439-0547	Massachusetts
Founders	525-2440	303-394-4404	Colorado
Ivy	456-5111	407-393-8900	Florida
Janus	523-8983	303-333-3863	Colorado
Neuberger & Berman	877-9700	212-476-8700	New York
T. Rowe Price	638-5660	410-547-2308	Maryland
Scudder	225-2470	617-439-4640	Massachusetts
Steinroe	338-2550	312-368-7800	Illinois
Strong	368-1030	414-359-1400	Wisconsin
20th Century	345-2021	816-531-5575	Missouri
Value Line	223-0818	212-687-3965	New York
Vanguard	662-7447	215-669-1000	Pennsylvania

TOTAL RETURN TEST

If you want to know the past performance of a fund, you can use a total return test. It's easy to use, and you can apply it to any fund. The total return of a fund stems from dividends and capital gains paid plus the change in the fund's price. When you combine these three items, you can compute a fund's total return or yield. Here's an illustration of how to determine a fund's total return.

Total Return Test
XYZ Fund

CATEGORY	AMOUNT
Dividends paid per share	$ 0.40
Capital gains distributions per share	$ 2.10
Subtotal	$ 2.50
Fund price at end of year	$24.00
Fund price at beginning of year	$20.00
Subtotal gain (loss) in fund price	$ 4.00

Totals:

Total return:	$6.50	($2.50 plus $4)
Total return percent:	32.5 percent	($6.50 divided by $20)

Once you determine a fund's total return, you can compare it to the return on other funds or the market indexes. Remember, even the best of funds may experience years when total return will not outperform the market indexes. However, the better funds will have more up than down years, and this is where to confine your selection.

INFORMATION SOURCES

Where can you find the information you need to select a fund? The place to begin is with the fund itself. Since a fund's prospectus contains its historical performance according to a standard format, it's easy to compare different funds. How do you get a prospectus? You can receive a prospectus by calling the fund and asking for one. Many libraries carry the addresses and telephone numbers of mutual funds.

In addition, many publications provide information on mutual funds. Here are some of them and what they cover.

Standard and Poor's Stock Guide furnishes statistical information on over seven hundred funds. This guide, issued monthly, contains a section on mutual funds. It includes the type of fund, such as growth, bond, income; the fund's total assets; high/low price per share for the last five years; minimum investment required; sales fees; the increase or decrease in value of an assumed $10,000 investment for funds during the last five years; and much more.

Investor's Business Daily devotes a section to mutual funds. In each issue, this newspaper includes 1990 to 1992 mutual fund performance rankings; percent of price change in 1993; current price; whether the fund is load or no-load; and the type of fund. The section also contains a feature article on funds and a mutual fund index that charts the performance of twenty funds.

Other sources of information include *Forbes* and *Business Week,* which once a year rank funds according to their performance, risk, and other factors. Also, *Morningstar's Mutual Fund Values, Weisenberger's Investment Companies, United Mutual Fund Selector,* and *Donoghue's Mutual Fund Almanac* issue information on funds.

SELECTING A FUND BY COMPUTER

If you have a personal computer, software packages can help you select a fund. The software can screen funds by variables such as load and no-load, 12b-1 fee, back-end load, annual expenses, risk, and annual return.

Here's a list of companies that offer software packages that will help you select a fund.

PROGRAM	TELEPHONE
Morningstar Mutual Funds Ondisc	312-427-1985
American Association of Individual Investors	312-280-0170
Rugg and Steele	310-914-1731
Business Week Mutual Fund Scoreboard	800-553-3575
Wealthbuilder	215-387-6055
Prodigy	800-776-0834

6

Dollar-Cost Averaging Plus

Successful investing in mutual funds is more a skill than a science. Success rests on examining several funds for investment, selecting the fund that promises the best return on your money, and considering new investment strategies for investing in the fund you select.

Dollar-Cost Averaging Plus (DCAP) is a new strategy for investing in mutual funds. DCAP is not a "get rich quick" scheme; rather, it is a long-term investment formula. It functions on the belief that the general trend of most mutual fund prices is up, and that within this trend, funds will experience both up and down price volatility. The DCAP formula requires that you increase investments when fund prices are relatively low and level off investments when their prices are high. One attractive aspect of the formula is that it relieves you of trying to decide when is the best time to invest in funds.

It requires little time and effort to apply the DCAP formula, and you don't have to be an expert on financial matters or mutual funds to use it. DCAP does not guarantee that you won't have losses, yet it could provide you with an above-average return on mutual funds.

Although the formula is an investment strategy that works best with mutual funds, you can also use it to buy individual shares of stock. Whether you use the formula to buy shares in funds or stocks, it can help you build that nest egg for college, provide a down payment for a house, supplement your retirement, or attain some other goal.

DEVELOPING THE DCAP FORMULA

There are many ways to invest in mutual funds. For example, typical dollar-cost averaging and lump-sum payment are two of the more popular ones. The DCAP formula is an effective refinement of the typical and often used strategy of dollar-cost averaging.

Several investment methods were tried before the DCAP formula began to take shape. As the formula evolved, issues had to be decided before it could be put to use.

The first issue was the selection of a fund. The DCAP formula provided a higher return when one of the better performing funds was selected. In addition, an even greater return was realized with a fund that had a wide high/low price range.

Since the formula required a target price to control the amount of each investment, it was important to set it as accurately as possible. It was best to set the target price in relation to the high/low price range of the fund. Also, it made little difference whether the target price was set to the fund's price range for a one-, two- or five-year period. This is simply because those funds that were good performers provided an above-average return almost every year.

Another issue was how much monthly investments should be increased if a fund's price dropped below the target price. This was resolved by correlating the amount of each investment to a maximum 25 percent drop allowed in a fund's price before investments stopped. Therefore, each 5 percent decrease in a fund's price below the target price required that investments be increased 20 percent to a maximum of 100 percent. As a rule, when the price of the better performing funds dropped below the target price, this usually created a buying opportunity.

The final issue concerned the reasons for ending investments should a fund drop sharply in price. Four reasons caused a fund to drop steeply in price: The fund had poor management, there was a change in the fund's management, the fund's investment philosophy or strategy changed, or general economic conditions badly deteriorated. When any of these occurred with a 25 percent drop in a fund's price, it was better to switch to another fund or invest temporarily in a money market mutual fund.

DCAP VS. TYPICAL
DOLLAR-COST AVERAGING

The typical method of dollar-cost averaging has been around for a long time and is one of the simplest ways to invest in mutual funds. It consists of investing a fixed amount of money in a fund at regular intervals. When you invest a fixed amount, fewer shares are bought when the fund is relatively high and more shares when it is low. The advantage of this method of investing is that the actual cost per share is usually less than the average price paid during the investment period.

In comparison, DCAP is a refinement of the typical method of dollar-cost averaging. The typical method requires that the amount you invest, whether at monthly, yearly, or other intervals, remains the same. DCAP requires that you invest monthly, and the amount of each investment varies in relation to a target price.

DCAP is an investment formula based on the assumption that the general trend of most mutual fund prices is up, but there will be both up and down price fluctuations in their rise. To take advantage of these fluctuations, DCAP requires that you set a target price to control the amount of your monthly investments. If your fund's price per share, its net asset value (NAV), drops below the target price, you increase the amount of your monthly investment. However, if your fund's price is higher than the target price, the amount of your investment stays the same.

In many ways DCAP is similar to typical dollar-cost averaging, but there are differences:

- With the DCAP formula, investments are monthly, while typical dollar-cost averaging requires investments monthly, quarterly, yearly, or at other intervals.
- The amount of DCAP investments can vary, while the amount of typical dollar-cost averaging investments remains constant.
- DCAP requires the setting and resetting of a target that determines the amount of each investment. Typical dollar-cost averaging does not require a target price.

COMPARISON OF DCAP WITH DOLLAR-COST AVERAGING

Any new investment strategy should prove that it is better than existing ways of investing. To see how the DCAP formula compares with typical dollar-cost averaging, let's invest in two imaginary funds.

We'll name the funds XYZ and ZYX-M. Both funds are the same except for one variable. Investments in XYZ Fund are according to the DCAP formula, and investments in ZYX-M Fund are consistent with typical dollar-cost averaging. ZYX-M has no target price, but XYZ has a $20 target price. Thus, if XYZ's price drops below the target price, the amount of the monthly investment increases.

When you compare the funds, note that the XYZ Fund using the DCAP formula provides a higher rate of return than typical dollar-cost averaging. The DCAP return is 15.3 percent and the typical dollar-cost averaging return 12.4 percent, a difference of almost 3 percent. A difference of 3 percent on an investment becomes a significant amount when you compound it for several years.

The initial investment in each fund was $500. Later investments in the XYZ Fund were in relation to the DCAP formula's target price and ranged from $100 to $160 a month. Investments in the ZYX-M Fund were held constant at $100 a month.

Dollar-cost Averaging Plus XYZ Fund

DATE OF INVESTMENT	DOLLAR AMOUNT OF INVESTMENT	COST PER SHARE	NUMBER OF SHARES BOUGHT	TOTAL SHARES
01-02-92	$500*	$20	25.000	25.000
02-03-92	$100	$21	4.761	29.761
03-03-92	$100	$22	4.545	34.306
04-03-92	$100	$20	5.000	39.306
05-04-92	$120	$19	6.315	45.621
06-03-92	$140	$18	7.777	53.398
07-03-92	$160	$17	9.411	62.809
08-03-92	$160	$17	9.411	72.720
09-03-92	$160	$17	9.411	82.131
10-02-92	$100	$20	5.000	87.131
11-03-92	$100	$21	4.761	91.892
12-03-92	$100	$22	4.545	96.437

Value of XYZ Fund on 12-03-92	$2,122
Dollar amount invested	$1,840
Dollar amount gain (loss)	$ 282
Rate of return	15.3 percent

*Initial investment.
Note: Table excludes capital gains and dividends.

The minimum monthly investment could be higher or lower than $100. If the minimum is $50, for example, the rate of return for both funds would be the same. The rate of return is what's important when comparing the two funds, not the amount you invest each month.

Remember, both funds are hypothetical and contain arbitrary figures, so there is no guarantee that you can earn a 15.3 percent or 12.4 percent return on your investment. Still, if you review the return on many funds, a 15.3 percent rate or even higher is possible.

Typical Dollar-cost Averaging ZYX-M Fund

Date of Investment	Dollar Amount of Investment	Cost Per Share	Number of Shares Bought	Total Shares
01-02-92	$500*	$20	25.000	25.000
02-03-92	$100	$21	4.761	29.761
03-03-92	$100	$22	4.545	34.306
04-03-92	$100	$20	5.000	39.306
05-04-92	$100	$19	5.263	44.569
06-03-92	$100	$18	5.555	50.124
07-03-92	$100	$17	5.882	56.006
08-03-92	$100	$17	5.882	61.888
09-03-92	$100	$17	5.882	67.770
10-02-92	$100	$20	5.000	72.770
11-03-92	$100	$21	4.761	77.531
12-03-92	$100	$22	4.545	82.076

Value of ZYX-M Fund on 12-03-92	$1,806
Dollar amount invested	$1,600
Dollar amount gain (loss)	$ 206
Rate of return	12.4 percent

*Initial investment.
Note: Table excludes capital gains and dividends.

Let's create another typical dollar-cost averaging fund and, instead of investing in it monthly, we'll invest semiannually. This fund we'll name ZYX-S.

When you review ZYX-S Fund, it's easy to see that investing semiannually with the typical method of dollar-cost averaging does have its defects. The return on the fund is only 5 percent. In comparison, XYZ Fund's return using the DCAP formula is 15.3 percent, or 10.3 percent higher. The low return on ZYX-S Fund is because one-half ($800) of the total investment was made when the fund was at its highest price of $22. When you compare ZYX-S Fund to XYZ Fund, it's apparent that investing monthly with the DCAP formula is the better method.

Typical Dollar-cost Averaging ZYX-S Fund

DATE OF INVESTMENT	DOLLAR AMOUNT OF INVESTMENT	COST PER SHARE	NUMBER OF SHARES BOUGHT	TOTAL SHARES
01-02-93	$800*	$20	40.000	40.000
12-03-93	$800	$22	36.363	76.363

Value of ZYX-S Fund on 12-03-93	$1,680
Dollar amount invested	$1,600
Dollar amount gain (loss)	$ 80
Rate of return	5 percent

*Initial investment.
Note: Table excludes capital gains and dividends.

DCAP'S COMPONENTS

When you invest according to the DCAP formula, there are four components to consider: initial investment, target price, amount of monthly investment, and maximum investment amount. To see how the formula's components function, let's look at this hypothetical investment.

Assume that you decide to invest in XYZ Growth Fund because it holds quality growth stocks, seems well-managed, and shows an average annual total return of 18 percent for the last five years. Moreover, after you satisfy the fund's initial investment requirement of $1,000, you decide to invest a minimum of $100 each month. Here's a rundown of DCAP's components and how they function in relation to your hypothetical fund.

Initial Investment

Your initial investment of $1,000 at $20 per share buys 50.000 shares in XYZ Fund. (The number of shares in mutual fund transactions are carried to three decimal places, which accounts for fractional ownership of shares.)

Target Price

To set the target price, let's assume that for the past five years the trading range of XYZ Fund was from a high of $22 to a low of $17, and its current price is $20. Since you feel that $20 is a fair price for the fund, you set that figure as your target price.

Monthly Investment Amount

As long as the price of XYZ Fund stays above the $20 target price, your monthly investments will be $100. Your investments will exceed $100 only if XYZ's price drops below the $20 target price.

The table below lists the amount of your monthly investments in relation to changes in the price of XYZ Fund. The table provides an easy way to determine the amount of your investments. Later in this chapter, there is a detailed example under the heading "How the DCAP Formula Works."

Monthly Investment Table XYZ Fund

TARGET PRICE	FUND'S PRICE PER SHARE	PERCENT OF FUND'S PRICE INCREASE OR DECREASE FROM TARGET PRICE	DOLLAR AMOUNT OF MONTHLY INVESTMENT
$20	$20	0	$100
$20	$19	−5	$120
$20	$18	−10	$140
$20	$17	−15	$160
$20	$16	−20	$180
$20	$15	−25	$200
$20	$16	−20	$180
$20	$17	−15	$160
$20	$18	−10	$140
$20	$19	−5	$120
$20	$20	0	$100
$20	$20	0	$100

All figures in the monthly investment table are rounded to the nearest dollar for simplicity. For example, if the XYZ's price is $19.50, it is rounded down to $19 as the basis for your monthly investment. Similarly, if the price is $19.51, it is rounded up to $20.

In the table, the amount of your investment varies in relation to the change of XYZ's price from the target price. During the investment period, the target price remains at $20. If you feel that the target price is set too high or too low, reset it using one of the other methods explained later in this chapter.

The minimum monthly investment in the table is $100. If you decide to set your minimum at $50, divide the last column in the monthly investment table by two, and the result is the amount of your investment. For example, if the fund's price is $17, a 15 percent drop from your target price, your monthly investment is $80. The main idea of the DCAP formula is the percent of increase or decrease of each investment, not the amount you decide to use as a base.

Maximum Investment Amount

There is a limit to your investments when XYZ Fund drops in price. Thus, each 5 percent drop in XYZ's price below the target price requires that you increase your monthly investment 20 percent, but only to a maximum of 100 percent. A 100 percent increase in your monthly investment correlates to a 25 percent drop in XYZ's price, and that great a decrease could indicate the fund has a problem.

THE TARGET PRICE

The target price determines the amount of your monthly investments. It is a trigger mechanism that rises or falls in relation to your fund's price. When accurately set, it could greatly increase the value of your investment in a fund.

To illustrate the function of the target price, let's suppose that you make an initial investment of $1,000 in a fund at $20 per share and plan to invest a minimum of $100 each month. Further, let's assume you feel that the fund's price of $20 is a good target price to determine the amount of future investments.

If the price of your fund drops to $19 (a 5 percent decrease), you increase the amount of your monthly investment by 20 percent, to $120. Similarly, if the price drops to $18 (a 10 percent decrease from the target price), you increase your monthly investment 40 percent, to $140. Thus, every 5 percent drop below the target price requires a 20 percent increase in your investment, to a total of 100 percent. If the price then rises from $18 to $20, the target price, your monthly investment would decrease from $140 to $100.

The base or minimum amount of the monthly investment used in this illustration is $100. Naturally, your base amount could be greater or less than $100. The amount should be what you can afford and still meet the minimum requirements of the fund.

SETTING THE TARGET PRICE

After you open an account with a fund, but before your first monthly investment, set the target price. There are various methods you can use to determine where to set the target price. Here's a rundown on the best methods to use.

Current Fund Price

You may set the target price at your cost per share when you open your account with a fund. In this case, if your initial cost is $20, your target price is $20, and monthly investments are in relation to the $20 target price. When you use your initial cost per share as the target price, you assume the fund is fairly valued at that price.

Median Price of Fund

Another way is to set the target price in relation to the high and low price range of your fund for the past year or multiple of years. For example, if the high/low range of your fund for the previous year was from $20 to $16, set the target price at $18, the median price. Similarly, if the range was from $20 to $14, set the target price at $17, again the median price.

Using the median price for a five- to ten-year period instead of for one year should give you a more accurate account of a fund's volatility, presumably in both up and down market cycles. To illustrate, let's say a fund's high/low range was from $24 to $16 for the last five years, the period you select to set the target price. In this case, set the target price at $20. All monthly investments in your fund are in relation to that price.

Market Indexes

Several indexes measure the stock market's performance. Three of the most widely used are the Dow-Jones Industrial Average, Standard and Poor's 500, and the NASDAQ Index. Suppose that you select the Dow-Jones Industrial Average for the past year to determine where to set your target price. If the Dow-Jones is 20 percent below its high for the past year, set your target price 20 percent below the fund's high price for the past year. Similarly, if you select the S&P 500, or the NASDAQ, set the target price the same percentage as the index is below its high price.

Before you select a market index, look at your fund's prospectus or quarterly reports and note which exchange lists most of the fund's stocks. Then select that exchange to set the target price. For example, if most of your fund's stocks are listed on the NASDAQ, choose the NASDAQ to set the target price.

There are several ways to set your fund's target price, and none of them is flawless. They are merely methods you can use to determine the amount of monthly investments. Of the methods discussed, probably the more accurate one is the median price of your fund for the past few years. This assumes that your fund has been in operation for the period you select.

HOW THE DCAP
FORMULA WORKS

Now that you are familiar with DCAP's components, let's look at the actual DCAP formula. To make the formula easy to apply, these alpha designations are used:

A = target price
B = fund price
C = target price less fund price
D = 20 percent variance multiplier
E = monthly investment increase
F = monthly investment base amount
G = total monthly investment

DCAP formula: A − B = (C × D) = (E + F) = G

The following is an example of how the DCAP formula works. In the example, the fund's trading range is $22 to $18, the target price is $20, and the minimum monthly investment is $100.

In the example of the DCAP formula, the target price remains at $20 during the investment period. When the fund's price is below the target price, the difference is multiplied by a 20 percent variance to arrive at the increase or decrease in the amount of your monthly investment.

Any increase in your monthly investment is added to the minimum monthly investment of $100 to determine your total investment. The minimum monthly investment could be higher or lower than $100 and the formula would not change.

Before each investment, compare your fund's price to the target price to determine the amount of your investment. You can get your fund's latest price from most large newspapers, the library, or by calling your fund.

DCAP Formula

A	− B	= (C	× D)	= (E	+ F)	= G
		TARGET PRICE LESS FUND PRICE	TIMES 20 PERCENT VARIANCE	MONTHLY INVEST- MENT INCREASE	MONTHLY INVEST- MENT BASE- AMOUNT	TOTAL MONTHLY INVEST- MENT
TARGET PRICE	FUND PRICE					
$20.00	$20.00	0	.20	0	$100	$100
$20.00	$18.55	$1.45	.20	$29	$100	$129
$20.00	$18.09	$1.91	.20	$38	$100	$138
$20.00	$17.52	$2.48	.20	$49	$100	$149
$20.00	$17.20	$2.80	.20	$56	$100	$156
$20.00	$16.94	$3.06	.20	$61	$100	$161
$20.00	$17.44	$2.56	.20	$51	$100	$151
$20.00	$18.28	$1.72	.20	$34	$100	$134
$20.00	$18.72	$1.28	.20	$26	$100	$126
$20.00	$19.50	$0.50	.20	$10	$100	$110
$20.00	$20.00	0	.20	0	$100	$100
$20.00	$22.09	0	.20	0	$100	$100
Totals				$354	$1,200	$1,554

RESETTING THE TARGET PRICE

There is good advice in the saying "if it works, don't fix it." You can apply the same reasoning to your fund's target price. There are only three reasons for you to reset the target price: when you set it in relation to the high/low price of your fund and your fund sets a new high price; when you set it in relation to one of the market indexes such as the Dow-Jones, Standard & Poor's, or the NASDAQ, and the index sets a new high price; and when your fund makes a distribution. If you plan to invest in your fund for the long term, say 10 to 15 years, you may have to reset the target price only a few times during that period.

Resetting the Target Price for New Highs

If you set the target price in relation to a fund's price and it sets a new high, the target price is reset. For example, let's suppose you invest in a fund with a price range from $24 to $20 and you set the target price at $22. Then the fund rises to a new high price of $25. In this case, reset the target price at $22.50, the median price. You can apply the same methodology when you use the Dow-Jones, S&P 500, or the NASDAQ Index as a reference to set the target price.

The target price is reset when your fund sets a new high price but not for a new low price, unless the new low occurs after a distribution, which is explained below. In case of a new low, monthly investments increase to a maximum of 100 percent from the target price, but the target price is not reset.

Resetting the Target Price for Distributions

There are two ways to receive distributions from your mutual fund—dividends and capital gains. When you receive distributions, the fund provides you with a statement that shows the date and dollar amount of the distribution, number of new shares purchased (if you reinvest your distributions in the fund), purchase price of the new shares, and the total shares you own. You can use the statement to help you determine if your fund's target price needs to be reset.

Since distributions reduce a fund's assets, the price of a fund is adjusted downward to reflect its new value. For example, if a fund's price is $21 the day before a distribution of $0.50, its price will decrease to $20.50 after the distribution. Because the securities held by the fund may increase or decrease in value the day of the distribution, they also must figure into the new price of the fund.

Taking the example a step further, suppose the securities held by a fund fell $0.50 on the distribution date. In that case, the new price of the fund is $20. You arrive at the $20 price by deducting $0.50 for the distribution and $0.50 for the decrease in the securities held by the fund from $21.

Let's look at the above example again and assume that the fund's trading range is $23 to $16 before the distribution, and the target price is $20. Since the price of the fund did not drop below the $20 target price on the distribution date, the target price is not reset.

Only when a distribution, within an increase or a decrease in a fund's price, changes the trading range is the target price reset. When you reset the target price after a distribution, usually it is to a lower figure and may require an increase in your monthly investments.

Let's take a situation where the price of your fund is $20, the trading range is from $21 to $19, and the target price is $20. Your fund then declares a $1.50 distribution, and on the distribution day the fund drops $0.50 in value. In this situation, the new trading range is $21 to $18 and the new target price is $19.50. This would require an increase of $30 to a $100 minimum monthly investment.

Determining Target Price for New Low After Distribution

Here's an example of how to determine the target price and amount to invest when your funds set a new low after a distribution.

Predistribution:

Trading range of fund	$21 to $19
Price of fund	$20
Target price	$20
Amount of monthly investment	$100
Amount of distribution	$1.50
Increase or decrease in fund price on distribution date	$0.50

Postdistribution:

Trading range of fund ($1.50 + $0.50 = $2 deducted from predistribution fund price of $20)	$21 to $18
Price of fund ($20 less $2)	$18
Target price (median price of new trading range)	$19.50
Amount of monthly investment (new target price of $19.50 less new fund price of $18 = $1.50 × 20 percent variance = $130)	$130

Determining Target Price for New
High After Distribution

Only rarely will a fund set a new high price on the day of a distribution. Should a new high occur on that day, reset the target price to reflect the fund's new trading range.

For example, let's imagine that a fund's trading range is $20 to $18, the target price is set at $19, and the current price of the fund is $19.50. The fund pays a distribution of $0.25 and rises $1 on the same date. In this situation, the fund set a new high at $20.25, and the new target price is $19.62. The new target price is determined by adding the $1 increase in the fund's price to $19.50 and deducting the $0.25 distribution. Then the fund's high price ($20.25) and low price ($18) are added and divided by two to arrive at $19.62.

The initial setting and then resetting of the target price is the key to greater profits when you use the DCAP formula. Be sure to examine the target price before each monthly investment, after distributions, and when your fund sets a new high.

CHECKING YOUR
FUND'S PERFORMANCE

As you would take your car in for an inspection or tune-up, you should periodically check your fund's performance. After you invest in your fund for about a year, check its total return. Total return measures your fund's performance based on the change in its share price and distributions.

To compute an approximate return, take the number of shares you own and multiply them by the current price of the fund. That will give you the market value of your shares. Next, add up the amount of your investments and subtract the total from the value of your shares. This will show whether your investment has increased or decreased in value.

You can divide the dollar amount of the increase or decrease by the amount of your investments to determine the percent of return.

Here's an illustration of how to figure your fund's total return. Let's say your fund is $20 at the beginning of the year and $22 when the year ends. During the year, it paid $0.80 a share in dividends and $1.60 a share in capital gains.

Price of fund at beginning of year	$20.00
Price of fund at end of year	$22.00
Increase in value of fund	$2.00
Dividends paid	$0.80
Capital gains paid	$1.60
Total return	$4.40
Total return rate ($4.40 divided by $20)	22 percent

To determine your fund's performance in relation to the market indexes, you can compare its total return to that of the Dow-Jones Industrial Average, S&P 500 Index, or the NASDAQ Index for the same period.

You will receive reports from your fund that show its return compared to one or more of the market indexes, usually the S&P 500. If your fund consistently underperforms the indexes, you should consider selling it. There is no reason to continue investing in a fund that doesn't regularly outperform the market indexes.

DCAP RESERVE FUND

It's a good idea to have a DCAP reserve fund in addition to your mutual fund. The reason for a reserve fund is to have money available to increase investments in your mutual fund when required by the DCAP formula. What's more, a reserve fund can serve as your emergency fund. If your mutual fund is part of a fund family, a money market fund usually is available to use as your reserve fund.

When you invest by the DCAP formula, monthly investments stop if your fund drops 25 percent in price. Should this occur, a reserve fund is a convenient place to invest the money that has been destined for your fund. The idea here is to keep in the habit of investing monthly. Later, when you decide whether to continue to invest in the same fund or switch to another, you can reinvest the money.

7

Investment Guidelines

Before you invest, set some guidelines. The most successful investors are those who have guidelines to follow. Besides helping you reach your goals, guidelines also give you the emotional satisfaction of knowing that you have put your financial plan to practical use.

Many newsletters and financial publications are ready to give you investment advice, usually at a fee. Some of the advice is good, but much is poor. When you have guidelines, it's much easier to determine which is the good advice and to make informed investment decisions. Here are some guidelines to consider before you invest.

SET INVESTMENT GOALS

Determine your goals before you make any investment decisions. Do you want to build a nest egg for your children's education? To provide for the down payment on a house? To supplement your retirement income? When you set goals, you take charge of your financial future.

INVEST IN MUTUAL FUNDS
FOR THE LONG TERM

When you invest in a mutual fund, consider it a long-term investment. The big gains in mutual funds usually are made by those who use a buy and hold strategy.

A few investors are fortunate enough to time their investments, being in a fund when its price is rising and selling before it drops. This involves the strategy of market timing that is not only difficult but also risky.

INVEST MONTHLY IN YOUR MUTUAL FUND

Mutual funds are especially attractive to people who want to invest each month. Moreover, if you invest all your money at one time, you stand the risk of paying too high a price for a fund. Monthly investments using the DCAP formula should provide a greater return on your money than one-time or sporadic investments in a fund. Investing monthly has another very good aspect—it gets you in the habit of saving.

AVOID EXCESSIVE FUND SWITCHING

It's usually not wise to use conversion privileges to switch in and out of funds randomly. Most studies show that trying to time the rise or fall of different funds is not as profitable as staying with one fund. The opportunity to switch funds is a useful service, but you should use it with discrimination.

BUY ONLY TOP PERFORMING NO-LOAD MUTUAL FUNDS

Which are the top performing no-load mutual funds? Chapter 5, "Selecting a Mutual Fund," answers that question. Keep in mind that some funds consistently do better than others. A fund's good performance record is not a guarantee that it will perform well in the future. Yet it's a good starting point for selecting a fund.

AVOID STEEP LOSSES ON MUTUAL FUNDS

Owning treasury securities guarantees that you will receive interest on your investment and your principal will be repaid at maturity. Owning shares in a mutual fund has no guarantee, and there is always the chance that you will lose a large part of your investment. Although some funds carry more risk than others, you can adopt safeguards so you won't lose all your money.

The DCAP formula, for example, limits losses by putting a cap on the amount of money you invest in a fund. When you invest by the DCAP formula, you can never lose more than 25 percent of your investment. In addition, the setting and resetting of the DCAP target price will make you aware of any continuous and significant decline in the price of your fund.

You can expect a certain amount of up and down price movement with a fund, but one that drops in price and remains down for a long period may have problems. In this case, it's usually best to sell the fund.

AVOID INDIVIDUAL BONDS

If you buy municipal or corporate bonds, invest in a bond mutual fund. Buying individual bonds can be risky. When you invest in a bond fund, your risk is reduced because you own a part of several bonds as opposed to a single bond that could drop significantly in price or default on its interest payments.

AVOID INVESTMENTS IN GOLD, SILVER, ART, AND COLLECTIBLES

Investments in precious metals, art, and collectibles carry a large amount of risk. Many people tout them as a hedge against inflation, but other investments with less risk can provide the same hedge.

DON'T GET INVOLVED IN SELLING SHORT, OPTIONS, AND COMMODITIES

Selling short, options, and commodities investments are risky, so usually it's better to avoid them. Few people consistently make money with selling short, options, or commodities.

DON'T BUY ON TIPS AND RUMORS

Don't listen to tips and rumors. This is probably difficult advice to follow, yet heeding rumors is the easiest way to lose money. The investment world is full of tips and rumors. Always check them out before you invest.

BUY ONLY QUALITY STOCKS

Quality stocks can be found in almost every industry. These stocks are industry leaders with sales and earnings that increase almost every year. They usually offer products or services with growth potential, pay dividends, and emphasize the development of new products or services. Their management is usually aggressive and experienced. These are the companies to consider if you invest in stocks.

SET A LOSS LIMIT

Before you invest in a stock, set a limit on the amount of loss you will tolerate should it drop in price. If you buy a stock at $20 a share, for example, limit any loss to 10 percent. In this case, you would sell the stock if it drops to $18. When you limit losses, it leaves most of your money available to buy another stock that may prove more lucrative.

HAVE AN EMERGENCY FUND

Before you invest, set aside about three months of your net income in a money market mutual fund or bank account for emergencies. There is no reason to own securities if you have to sell them for emergencies.

DEBT MANAGEMENT

If you have debt, don't invest until it's under control. It makes no sense to start an investment program when you have excessive debt. If you use over 20 percent of your net income for charge and credit card payments, you may have too much debt.

BEFORE YOU INVEST, CHECK YOUR INSURANCE PROGRAM

It's to your advantage to have adequate life, health, accident, and mortgage coverage before you invest. The amount of your insurance depends on your age, the number and age of your dependents, and your health.

OPEN AN INDIVIDUAL RETIREMENT ACCOUNT, KEOGH PLAN, OR OTHER RETIREMENT PLAN

If you are eligible, contribute to a tax-deferred retirement plan. It's surprising how quickly tax-deferred investments can increase in value when compared to those that are taxable.

BUILD YOUR INVESTMENT PORTFOLIO GRADUALLY

Whether you have a relatively large amount to invest or only a few hundred dollars, it's usually better to move slowly when you start to invest. This requires investing bit by bit rather than a large amount at one time. For example, if you plan to put $1,500 in a stock, invest it in increments of $500 a few weeks apart.

DIVERSIFY YOUR INVESTMENT PORTFOLIO

A diversified portfolio holds more than one investment. For instance, you could invest in a mutual fund, stocks, bonds, and a money market fund. With a diversified portfolio, you lessen your risk should one type of investment not prove profitable.

BE AN INFORMED INVESTOR

With the large amount of financial publications available, you can easily obtain information about investments.

Although knowledge doesn't guarantee success, it may help you make better investment decisions and avoid losses.

To become an informed investor, you should do more than occasionally read the financial pages in the local newspaper. You need to have an understanding of investment basics and the securities markets.

Some newspapers that publish financial information are *Investor's Business Daily*, *The Wall Street Journal*, and *Barron's*. Magazines that provide business and investment information include *Forbes*, *Business Week*, *Fortune*, and *Money*.

In addition, *Standard and Poor's Stock Guide* contains statistical information on stocks and mutual funds. The *Value Line Investment Survey* provides analysis and recommendations on 1,700 stocks.

A good way to learn about specific stocks is to write for a company's annual report, which is free of charge. If you have questions about the report, you can call the company and sometimes talk to a financial officer.

Other ways you can learn about investments include enrolling in an investment course at a local school and checking with the nearest library for information.

It's to your advantage to set some guidelines before you invest. They don't have to be complex—just basic rules to follow. As you gain investment experience, you will probably add more guidelines to the above list. The important point is to have guidelines and stick with them.

8

Building Your Portfolio

A portfolio is the total of all your salable items. This includes property such as stocks, bonds, mutual funds, real estate, art, bank accounts, and money market funds. For example, your portfolio may contain a mutual fund, money market fund, two stocks, a bank account, and the equity in your home, with a total value of $80,000.

Contrary to what some people think, there is nothing complex about building and managing your portfolio. If you follow the suggestions in this book, you can do it easily.

Before you earmark any money for new investments, look at your current investments. Are you satisfied with them? Do they carry too much risk for you? Do they provide a good return on your money? Once you decide this, match the return you expect and your risk level with available investments. This way you can shape a portfolio that you will feel comfortable with.

DIVERSIFICATION

All investments carry a degree of risk. One way to reduce risk is to diversify your portfolio by holding more than one type of investment. If you put all your money in one investment, you could suffer a big loss should something go wrong. Even if you have only a small amount of money to invest, allocate it among more than one investment to reduce your risk.

When you invest in a growth mutual fund, you get immediate diversification. That's because a growth fund holds a variety of securities such as stocks, bonds, and cash equivalents. If you also invest in a money market fund, government securities, and a bond fund, your portfolio would be even more diversified and less risky.

Diversification does not mean investing in as many different types of securities as possible, but selecting a few that are not too risky and yet have the potential to provide a good return on your money.

PORTFOLIO VARIABLES

You should consider some variables before you start your portfolio. The first is your age. Usually, the younger you are the more speculative the investments you can hold in your portfolio. If you are close to retirement age, your portfolio probably should be more conservative.

Another variable is your occupation. If your income is uncertain or varies from year to year, your portfolio should contain less risky investments than that of someone with an income that is steadily increasing.

The number of dependents in your family and the amount of your debt also should influence the way you shape your portfolio. A single person with no debts can usually hold more speculative investments than someone who has three children, car payments and a house mortgage.

ASSET ALLOCATION PLANS

Asset allocation is the method that determines how you divide your portfolio among different investments. It apportions your portfolio into different investment groups but does not show you which securities to hold in your portfolio. For example, what portion of your portfolio is going to be invested in mutual funds, stocks, bonds, and cash?

Although asset allocation plans vary among individuals, yours could take the shape of one of the following plans for an assumed $5,000 investment—the amount of your investment, of course, can be larger or smaller than $5,000.

Asset Allocation Plans

PLAN #1

TYPE OF INVESTMENT	DOLLAR AMOUNT INVESTED	PERCENT OF INVESTMENT
Money market mutual fund	$3,750	75 percent
Growth mutual fund	$1,250	25 percent
Total	$5,000	100 percent

PLAN #2

TYPE OF INVESTMENT	DOLLAR AMOUNT INVESTED	PERCENT OF INVESTMENT
Money market mutual fund	$1,000	20 percent
Growth mutual fund	$2,500	50 percent
Common stocks	$1,000	20 percent
Series EE bonds, zero-coupon bonds, corporate or municipal bonds	$ 500	10 percent
Total	$5,000	100 percent

PLAN #3

TYPE OF INVESTMENT	DOLLAR AMOUNT INVESTED	PERCENT OF INVESTMENT
Money market mutual fund	$1,000	20 percent
Growth fund or growth and income fund	$1,500	30 percent
Common stocks	$1,000	20 percent
U.S. government bond fund, corporate bond fund or municipal bond fund	$1,500	30 percent
Total	$5,000	100 percent

Asset allocation plan #1 is a conservative investment approach, primarily for the beginning investor—usually the person just out of high school or college. The plan has the potential to provide a good total return with the investment in a growth fund. Yet a large percentage of the $5,000 is invested in a money market mutual fund as a reserve for future investments.

Plan #2 is for the person who has been employed for a few years and has decided that it's time to consider college for the children, a bigger home, or income to supplement retirement. While the plan is moderately conservative, it still has more growth potential than plan #1. The percentage in a money market mutual fund is less than in plan #1, enough to cover an emergency situation. Plan #2 has the potential to fulfill medium- to longer-term goals.

Plan #3 is for the person who has well-defined investment goals—the person with enough experience and confidence in investing that he or she can take an aggressive investment approach, and yet maintain a relatively risk-free portfolio. This plan is probably suitable for someone nearing or in retirement.

These asset allocation plans will not fit the requirements of all investors. Among the three plans, there can be considerable overlapping of investments. For example, though you might be a beginning investor, there is no reason you can't invest in stocks. But the plans will give you an idea of how asset allocation works.

There are two investments in the allocation plans that you should consider for your portfolio. These are growth funds and common stocks. They have been discussed earlier, but deserve further review because they are relatively safe investments and generally provide an above-average return.

GROWTH MUTUAL FUNDS

Growth funds usually are good long-term investments for an asset allocation plan. They can preserve your purchasing power against erosion from inflation and have the potential to provide a good return. They are especially appropriate when saving for college, housing, or retirement. After an emergency fund, you should consider a growth fund as your next investment.

Growth funds are good investments because they have most of their assets in growth stocks and the remainder in bonds and cash equivalents for income and defensive purposes. In short, they are diversified. Yet they have the potential to provide a good return.

Growth funds place more emphasis on capital gains and less importance on the payment of dividends. Since it's possible to earn a 15 percent to 20 percent average annual total return investing in growth funds, probably no other investment can match their long-term appeal.

If you are a long-term investor, don't let the day-to-day fluctuations of a growth fund disturb you. Time and the reinvestment of dividends and capital gains usually provide a good return. The secret for a good return on a growth fund is to invest regularly for a long period, and reinvest all dividends and capital gains paid by the fund to buy additional shares.

COMMON STOCKS

If it's wealth you want, then quality common stocks belong in your portfolio. Stocks offer the greatest potential return on your investment dollars. If you invest in stocks, it's to your advantage to know how the stock market works and to have investment guidelines.

When you buy shares of stock, you own a part of a company. The amount of your ownership depends on the number of shares you hold and the number of shares issued by the company. For example, if you own two thousand shares and the company has issued 10 million shares, your ownership is 0.2 percent.

As a stockholder, you share in any company profits—and losses. When there are profits, you could realize an increase in the price of your stock and the payment of dividends. Yet there is no guarantee that a stock will increase in price above what you paid for it, or pay a dividend.

Since stocks can have wide price fluctuations, you may find them hard to deal with. There can be periods when stock prices fall substantially. However, over the long term, stocks generally provide attractive and competitive returns.

Capital Gains

Capital gains occur when the proceeds from the sale of a stock exceed the cost of buying a stock. For example, suppose you bought one hundred shares of XYZ Company at $20 a share and sold it two years later for $35. In this case, your capital gains are $15, less brokerage commissions for buying and selling the stock.

You must report all capital gains to the IRS for the tax year you receive them, and they are taxed at your current tax bracket rate. If you are in the 28 percent tax bracket, then you pay 28 percent of your capital gains to the IRS.

To some people, the taxes on capital gains may seem excessive. Nevertheless, stocks are taxed at the same rate as interest earned on savings accounts, money market mutual funds, bonds, and most other investments.

Dividends

The regular payment of a dividend increases the attractiveness of a stock. Although a company is not required to pay a dividend, dividends usually are paid when a company has good sales and earnings growth. Others pay a large percentage of their profits to shareholders. A company's board of directors determines the amount of the dividend that usually is paid quarterly.

A company can pay its stockholders two kinds of dividends: cash and additional shares of stock. A cash dividend is the stockholder's share of the company's profits. You can determine the yield (return) on a company's cash dividend by dividing the current price of the stock into the annual dividend payout. For instance, a stock priced at $20 that pays a yearly dividend of $1 yields 5 percent. Thus, you can compare a stock's yield to the interest paid on bank savings accounts, bonds, and other investments to determine which has the better return.

When a company issues additional shares of stock to its shareholders, that is called a stock dividend or simply a stock split. For example, if you own one hundred shares and a company splits its stock two for one, you have two hundred shares after the split. It's like trading a $10 bill for two $5 bills. Since all shareholders participate in the split, your percentage of ownership in the company is the same. And the value of your investment does not change, since the new shares would be half the price of the pre-split shares. Some companies issue stock dividends with or instead of cash dividends.

If you invest in common stocks, it's a good idea to consider closely a company's dividend record. Pay special attention to the dividend yield, frequency of increases (or decreases) in the dividend during the previous ten years, and any stock splits which can indicate a company's sales and earnings are increasing.

Dividend Reinvestment Plans

A high percentage of the companies that pay cash dividends have dividend reinvestment plans (DRPs) that are attractive to many of their shareholders. DRPs allow shareholders to reinvest all or part of their cash dividends to purchase additional shares of the company's stock, sometimes at a 3 percent to 5 percent discount from the stock's market price. In addition, many DRPs allow shareholders to make cash investments to buy additional shares of the company's stock. You can sell all or part of your shares back to the company at any time.

It's easy to join a DRP. All you do is call for a company's DRP prospectus and enrollment application. Complete the application and return it to the company. However, before you can enroll in a DRP, you have to buy shares in the company through a stockbroker. What this means is that most companies with DRPs do not handle an initial stock purchase directly.

WORKING WITH A BROKERAGE FIRM

Regardless of the amount of money that you have to invest, you will be welcome when you contact a brokerage firm. If you are a beginning investor, know what you want before you contact a brokerage. If you know in advance what you expect, you save time and you will not be investing in something that doesn't interest you.

Full-Service vs. Discount Brokerage Firms

There are two kinds of brokerage firms: full-service and discount. The full-service brokers, as their name implies, offer a wide range of financial services to their clients. They make, buy, sell, and hold recommendations on stocks and other investments; provide research information on specific securities; and offer portfolio guidance to their clients.

The discount brokers, on the other hand, neither furnish their clients with research nor provide investment advice. They primarily execute buy and sell orders. Since discount brokers offer fewer services than full-service brokers, they charge much lower commissions. Discount brokers' commissions can be 50 percent to 70 percent less than those for full-service brokers.

It's not surprising that discount brokers cater to clients who prefer to make their own decisions. If you follow the suggestions in this book, you can make your own investment decisions. Thus, a discount broker is all you need. However, if you want someone to hold your hand, a full-service broker may be better for you.

Mutual Funds and Brokerage Firms

You can purchase mutual funds through discount as well as full-service brokers. But full-service brokers sell exclusively load funds, while discount brokers, such as Charles Schwab, handle both load and no-load funds.

You can buy shares in a no-load fund yourself, without the service of a full-service or discount broker. When you don't have the time, or if you have problems with a fund's prospectus, then buy a no-load fund through a discount broker.

TIMING MUTUAL FUND INVESTMENTS

When is the best time to invest in mutual funds? The typical answer is to invest in them when the prime interest rate (the preferential rate of interest on short-term loans by banks to their most creditworthy customers) is relatively low. When the prime rate is high, funds usually move down in price, and they rise when rates are low or going down. There is, of course, no proven method to determine when rates are at their peak or when they reach bottom.

At times you may be tempted to act on fluctuations in the price of a mutual fund. You could convince yourself to sell a fund when its price drops, then reinvest in the same fund when its price starts to rise. This is called timing the market, a skill that few investors have. If your fund drops in price, it's better to stay invested and let timing be the concern of your fund's manager.

One advantage of the DCAP formula is that it compensates you for any poorly timed investments in a mutual fund. Thus, don't let interest rates or a fund's price dictate when you will invest in a fund. Rather, make your first investment when you have the money and follow up with monthly investments using the DCAP formula.

PORTFOLIO CHECKUP

As a motor tune-up can keep your car in good running condition, a review of your portfolio can keep it in shape. However, a review of your portfolio doesn't always mean it has to be overhauled.

It's a good practice to check your mutual fund monthly rather than daily. With a daily checkup, you could overreact to a short-term fluctuation in price. It's not a big job to check your fund's performance. After each investment, the fund will send you a financial statement that shows the number of shares you purchased, the purchase price, and total shares you own. The statement includes enough information so you can check your fund's performance.

Since stocks are more risky investments than mutual funds, it's a good idea to check them daily. Any 10 percent decline in a stock below your purchase price is cause for concern.

Once you gather the information on your portfolio's performance, what do you do with it? First, compare the return on the investments in your portfolio with similar types of investments. For example, compare the performance of your mutual fund with that of the S&P 500 or another market index. Compare the return on your money market mutual fund with a money market deposit account at a bank. In short, compare your portfolio's return to similar investments and what you could have earned investing in them for the same period. If your return is less than that for comparable investments, maybe it's time to change the holdings in your portfolio.

SPECIAL CONSIDERATIONS

Starting Small

Contrary to what some people believe, you don't need a lot of money to start your portfolio. In fact, it could be to your advantage to begin with a relatively small amount. That way, as you invest, you will gain experience that could prevent later losses.

Consistency

One criterion for a high return on a mutual fund is to invest regularly. Before you buy shares in a fund, determine the amount of money you can afford to invest each month. And once you begin to invest in a fund, stick with it.

Patience

When you invest in a growth mutual fund, patience can be your greatest ally. Usually, you should consider a growth fund as a long-term investment. In the short run, the price of a growth fund can be volatile, and it can fluctuate with stock prices in general. The best strategy is to buy and hold even if the price of your fund drops for a while. Think of your fund the same way as you would a house. Seldom would you sell your house because of a short-term drop in house prices.

Revising Your Portfolio

Deciding on an asset allocation plan for your portfolio is not a one-time project. You should revise your plan for each stage of your life. The asset mix for someone who is single is different from that of a married person with children ready for college. For example, when your children are nearing college age, it's time to start selling your more risky investments and placing the proceeds in safer money market funds, treasury bonds, and other fixed-income securities. And as you approach retirement age, you may want less money in stocks and more in bond funds for safety and income.

Recordkeeping

It's important that you keep good records on the investments in your portfolio. They will come in handy for tax purposes. When you buy or sell securities, enter all pertinent information, such as the date of the transaction, number of shares bought or sold, the price, and any commission costs, in a log. As a shareholder in a fund or stock, you own a part of the business, and good records are an essential part of doing business.

9

Total Financial Plan

A total financial plan covers all your family's needs. It includes family requirements such as money set aside for emergencies, adequate insurance, housing, college expenses, retirement, estate planning, and your investments. As a rule, a total plan is usually not built all at once. Rather, you develop it steadily through the years as your family needs dictate and money becomes available.

If you are just starting your financial plan, you probably have to stretch your paycheck to cover monthly expenses. In this case, you should set priorities on which of your family's needs are the most important. Certainly, two of your top priorities should be to set money aside for emergencies and to provide adequate insurance for yourself and your family. After you cover these, the next priority will, of course vary among individuals. For some, saving for the down payment on a house is next. Others may want to invest for their children's education. Once you have set your priorities, model your portfolio to attain them. Here are some family needs to consider when you set your priorities.

EMERGENCY FUND

There's no reason to have a financial plan until you have money set aside for unexpected emergencies. Where you invest your emergency money can make a difference. It's better to put your emergency dollars in a money market mutual fund than a passbook savings account. A money market fund is more attractive since it pays a higher return and is more difficult to draw on than a savings account.

LIFE INSURANCE

Before you invest, make sure that you have adequate life insurance. How do you determine if the insurance you have is enough? The answer, of course, is to look at your family's needs and the amount of insurance you have now.

Think of life insurance as the way to maintain your family's living standard should something happen to you. If something does happen, most financial experts agree that your family would need about 75 percent of its current net income to maintain the same living standard. When you figure your family's needs, include social security benefits and the cost of your children's education.

Maybe you have too much life insurance. Some people buy more insurance than they actually need. Few people without children need a large amount of life insurance. Insurance is for protection, whether for the loss of a family head or a business. So buy it as a protection against financial loss and not as an investment.

There are two basic kinds of life insurance: term and whole life. Let's look at them to see what they have to offer.

Term Insurance

Term insurance only provides death protection, and cash value is not built up. Over a short period, term insurance provides the most coverage at the least amount possible. However, the premiums (the cost) of term insurance increase substantially with your age until coverage is very costly when you are ready for retirement. Even so, many term policies are convertible, which means you can switch to a whole life policy later on.

Whole Life Insurance

Whole life not only provides you with protection but also has a savings feature that allows you to build up cash value. With whole life, the premiums remain constant throughout your lifetime. Although whole life is more expensive than term when you are young, at retirement age whole life insurance is the less expensive.

In the last few years, universal life, which is a hybrid type of whole life, has become popular. In this kind of policy, you receive life protection and at the same time build up cash value that is tax-deferred.

The type of life insurance that most people really need varies. The single person may not need any insurance. The married person with no children may need only a small term policy. A person with a family may need term insurance that is convertible to a whole life policy later on.

Buying Insurance

When you buy life insurance, be careful. Within the last few years, some insurance companies have had financial problems. This raises the question, What if I outlive the insurance company? Fortunately, you can take some precautions to improve your chances of avoiding an insurance company that's shaky.

First, know which insurance company is behind the policy you are considering. Then check the company's credibility in either *Best's Insurance Reports*, *Standard and Poor's*, *Moody's*, or *Duff and Phelps*. These publications, available at most libraries, rate insurance companies according to their financial strength. Always purchase your insurance from a financially strong company.

Second, consider whether to diversify by buying policies from two or three different companies instead of a large policy from one company, thus reducing your risk.

Finally, if you have group coverage at work, it's probably better to get your insurance there—assuming that your employer has chosen a financially strong insurance company.

HOUSING

Whether you own a home or rent, housing is an important part of any investment program. Keep in mind that a house is first a place to live and then an investment. What's more, a house is not a liquid investment. At times, it can be almost impossible to sell a house at the asking price.

During the 1970s and 1980s, the prices of many houses increased in value. However, the boom in real estate has leveled off and even gone down in some states as more potential homeowners are finding housing unaffordable.

Whether or not you are a homeowner, here are some advantages and disadvantages to owning a home.

- A house can provide security and stability. When you rent there is always the chance that you may have to move.
- A house usually has more living space than an apartment and fewer restrictions.
- There are financial benefits when you own a house since property taxes and mortgage interest are tax deductible. If you sell your house, any capital appreciation would go to you. What's more, you can defer any capital appreciation when you sell a house and buy another one of equal or greater value within a specified period.
- Owning a house brings a feeling of satisfaction to many people.
- There is no guarantee that you can sell your house for more than its purchase price.
- When you rent, your money is not tied up in a down payment on a house.
- If you are a homeowner, there will be maintenance costs such as roof repairs, painting, electrical repairs and other upkeep.

The decision of whether to rent or buy a house is primarily a matter of personal preference and available resources. If you don't expect to live in a house more than three to five years, renting is usually more economical than buying.

INVESTING FOR COLLEGE

It's no secret that college is expensive, and the price is likely to continue to rise. The average tuition at a public college today is about $5,000 to $6,000 a school year. With college costs rising about 5 percent to 6 percent a year, fifteen years from now the cost could be as high as $11,000 to $12,000 for a school year.

You can't rely too much on financial aid such as grants, scholarships, and student loans to pay for college expenses. These programs frequently have eligibility requirements that not all students and their families can meet.

Before the Tax Reform Act of 1986, Clifford trusts could be used to help families pay for college by shifting income to someone, usually a child, in a lower tax bracket than the parents. Although tax reform ended many tax breaks, it's still possible to save for college by opening a custodial account under the Uniform Gifts to Minors Act (UGMA).

Under the UGMA, if you are the custodian, you can manage the assets of your child's account. If your child is under age fourteen, the first $500 of yearly interest, dividends, and capital gains is not taxed at the federal level. If your child is age fourteen or older, the first $500 of interest, dividends, and capital gains is not subject to federal income taxes, and any amount over $500 is taxed at the child's rate. It's possible to set up a custodial account with most mutual funds and discount brokers such as Charles Schwab or Fidelity. They provide a choice of investments and handle most of the paperwork.

Develop an Investment Plan

The most obvious way to ensure the availability of money for your children's education is to set up a college investment plan. This involves estimating the cost of your children's college expenses, projecting the amount of your income to the time they are ready for college, determining how much money you can get from scholarships and loans, and deciding how much of your current income is available for college investments. The sooner you set up a plan, the easier your task will be.

Investment Suggestions

If your children are under age fourteen, investing in a growth mutual fund is a good way to pay for college costs. When your children are older, you probably shouldn't commit college money to a growth fund. So that is the time to switch from a growth fund to a money market fund or high rated zero-coupon bonds that mature about the time your children are ready to enter college.

A number of states offer tax-exempt zero-coupon bonds for in-state people saving for college expenses. Most of the zero-coupon college bonds that states offer are general obligation bonds and carry high safety ratings. These bonds are sold through brokers, not directly to investors.

Series EE savings bonds provide a safe investment for college-designated money. Although their return is a relatively low 4 percent if held for five years, you can redeem Series EE bonds tax-free at maturity, provided the money goes toward college tuition and your income falls within certain limits.

There are other ways to raise money for college, such as taking out a home equity loan, borrowing on your life insurance, or creating a trust, but using these assets might shortchange other family needs.

RETIREMENT

It's never too early to start investing for retirement. Since a comfortable retirement isn't something that just happens, you should begin investing for it several years before you leave your job.

How much will you need to live comfortably in retirement? Many people say it will require about 75 percent of the income you earn before retirement to maintain an equivalent standard of living. After retirement, housing, clothing, transportation, and taxes will probably be less, but medical expenses may be higher.

Where will you get your retirement income? For most people, it will originate from a company pension plan, social security, and personal investments. If you have a company pension, it will cover about 50 percent to 60 percent of your retirement expenses. If you are eligible for social security, it will cover even less. That means, for a comfortable retirement, you will have to start saving for it before you retire. Here are descriptions of the more popular retirement plans.

Social Security

Social security provides monthly payments for life to qualifying wage earners. It pays some on Medicare costs, reduces benefits for people retiring early, and reduces payments to those who earn more than a specified amount in retirement. You must contribute to social security for at least forty quarters or the equivalent of ten years to be eligible for benefits. Since social security probably won't cover all your expenses in retirement, you will need other sources of income.

401(K) Plan

The 401(K) is one of the best retirement plans available. The plan, set up by your employer, is tax-deferred until you make withdrawals. Since you can deduct your contributions to the plan from your salary, you pay less income taxes. Your employer also may contribute to your 401(K), either with a matching contribution or with a profit-sharing plan.

Many 401(K)s offer participants a choice of investments and the chance to change them. Also, some plans offer the choice of growth and fixed-income investments, and others offer mutual funds. In many 401(K) plans, participants can borrow against their investment to purchase a principal residence. Since the 401(K) is a good way to save for retirement, take advantage of it if you have the opportunity.

Keogh Plan

If you are self-employed, you can open a tax-deferred Keogh plan for your retirement. There are two types of Keogh plans: defined-benefit and defined-contribution. The main difference between the two is that the defined-contribution plan sets limits on what goes in your account, while the defined-benefit plan has no limitation. Which of these plans is better for you depends on your age and other factors. If you set up a Keogh, you must designate a trustee, such as a mutual fund, brokerage firm, or bank, to administer the plan.

Like the 401(K) plan, a Keogh plan offers tax-deferred savings until you withdraw them and the opportunity to deduct contributions from your taxable income. Your contributions to a Keogh are limited to a dollar amount or percentage of your annual income.

Since a Keogh is an ideal way for you to save for retirement and reduce your taxable income, make a full contribution to one if you qualify.

Simplified Employee Pension

The Simplified Employee Pension (SEP) combines the main features of an individual retirement account (IRA) and a Keogh plan. If you are self-employed, you can open a SEP or your employer can open one if you qualify. If your employer opens a SEP for you, it could be linked to the firm's profits as a pension and profit-sharing plan. The contributions you make to a SEP are vested and not taxable income until withdrawn.

You may also contribute to a SEP-IRA. These contributions are tax-deductible, and you pay no income tax on them until they are withdrawn. Individuals who are self-employed may also contribute to a SEP-IRA rather than a Keogh plan.

Individual Retirement Account

IRAs are available to all wage earners whether or not they have another pension plan. You can invest up to $2,000 yearly in an IRA. If you are married and you and your spouse both work, you may invest a total of $4,000 yearly. If only one spouse works, you may invest $2,250 each year.

If neither you nor your working spouse is covered by an employer retirement plan, both of you can take a full IRA deduction of up to $2,000 or 100 percent of earned income, whichever is less. Though you may have a pension plan at work, you can still make a fully deductible IRA contribution if your income doesn't exceed $25,000 if single and $40,000 if married. Single people who earn between $25,000 and $35,000 and married people who earn between $40,000 and $50,000 may qualify for a partial tax deduction.

As it turns out, IRAs are good investments because your assets grow tax-deferred until you withdraw them. For example, if you invest $200 a month in an IRA, and receive an 8 percent rate of return, you will accumulate around $117,000 after twenty years. The minimum age at which you can receive payments from an IRA is 59½, unless there are special circumstances such as disability. Withdrawals must start by age 70½.

There are three basic types of IRAs: individual retirement account, or contributory; individual retirement annuity; and trust account set up by employers or employee associations, which was covered earlier in this chapter under the SEP.

Individual Retirement Account
or Contributory IRA

This is the main type of IRA that you establish as a trust or custodial account. The trustee or custodian must be an organization such as a brokerage firm, mutual fund, bank, credit union, or insurance company and usually charges initial and yearly account fees of $25 to $50 for its services.

The amount of flexibility that you have in an individual IRA depends on where you establish your account. For example, a brokerage firm can set up an IRA for you to invest in stocks, bonds, mutual funds, money market funds, and other types of investments. However, you cannot invest IRA money in artworks, antiques, rare gems, metals, collectibles, or life insurance.

Individual Retirement Annuity

An individual retirement annuity is actually an IRA endowment contract that insurance companies offer. This type of annuity also can be combined with life insurance.

At age 59½ an individual retirement annuity allows you either lifetime payments or a lump-sum withdrawal of your money. The problem with these options is that payments are at a fixed rate and thus subject to erosion by inflation.

ANNUITY

An annuity is actually an investment contract in which you as the policyholder receive payments for life or a fixed period. It's your decision how much and how often you contribute to an annuity. As strange as it seems, annuities are sold through insurance companies. However, many mutual funds and brokerage firms also sell annuities, but only in conjunction with insurance companies. There are two basic kinds of annuities: immediate and tax-deferred.

Immediate Annuity

With an immediate annuity, you pay the insurer a lump sum of money and receive a fixed monthly amount during your lifetime. The amount you receive depends on your age, sex, amount of your investment, and the total years you select to receive the income. With an immediate annuity, it's a good idea to name a beneficiary to receive the income in case of your death. Although a beneficiary reduces the amount of the annuity, if you die soon after you buy the annuity without naming a beneficiary, the insurer receives the income.

Tax-Deferred Annuity

A tax-deferred annuity is a contract that allows you to invest tax-free until you receive payments at a later date. You can buy a tax-deferred annuity either by installments or with a lump-sum payment. There are two types of tax-deferred annuities: fixed and variable.

The fixed annuity guarantees a fixed yield for a certain period, usually one to five years. After that, the insurer guarantees only a lower yield.

As the name implies, a variable annuity pays a varying amount to the policyholder when withdrawals begin after age 59$\frac{1}{2}$. This type of annuity gives you a choice of investment options, primarily different kinds of mutual funds.

The advantages to tax-deferred annuities are that your investments are tax-free until you make withdrawals, and you avoid probate since they are insurance policies.

The disadvantages are that you cannot cash in annuities prematurely without a penalty; they have high management fees and surrender charges; taxes on them are only postponed, not canceled; and the managers of annuities may make bad investments with your money that could affect the yield on your annuity.

If you plan to buy an annuity, remember that there are no risk-free investments, and annuities are no exception to this rule. Like real estate companies and banks, life insurance companies have also had their financial troubles. Although most life insurance companies in the United States are healthy, some people question whether all of their pension annuities will remain sound.

What's happened to the annuities of insurance companies? In some cases, the insurance companies that are in trouble have invested heavily in junk bonds that have decreased in price or defaulted and in speculative real estate that has decreased in value. Insurance companies have placed their clients' money in these investments for a higher yield to attract more customers and in the process took on more risk.

Remember, your annuity is only as safe as the insurance company that issues it. There is no federal program to cover insurance losses as there is with bank accounts and stocks. You may do as well investing the same amount of money on your own rather than buying an annuity.

ESTATE PLANNING

Once you set up your financial plan, consider an estate plan to transfer your assets to your beneficiaries should anything happen to you. An estate plan ensures that your estate will be distributed according to your wishes.

You'll probably find that an estate plan will require adjustments from time to time to reflect changes in your family situation. And you will need the help of an adviser such as an attorney or banker to make it legal. If you plan to see an adviser, make a list of your assets and determine their value. Then decide how you want your assets distributed. This way, you can save time and money.

Making a Will

Regardless of the amount of your assets, you should have a will. If you die intestate, without a will, what will happen to your estate? A court in your state will appoint someone to distribute your assets. If you are married, it would probably be your surviving spouse. If you were the surviving spouse, one of your children would probably distribute your assets. If there is no relative to distribute your estate, the court would appoint a public administrator. In that case, your estate is divided among your relatives.

When you make a will, you must name an executor for your estate. The executor is responsible for distributing your assets as you direct and administering other aspects of your will. You could name your surviving spouse or another family member as the sole executor, or you can have two or more executors—for instance, your spouse or another relative as co-executor with an attorney or bank. The executors of an estate receive a fee, set by state law, that usually ranges between 1 and 3 percent of the estate's value.

An estate for which there are children or elderly dependents could require an executor for several years. During this period, the executor might be unable to continue to administer your estate. In that case, you should name a successor executor at the time you draw up your will. If a successor executor isn't named, the court would appoint one who might not handle your estate as you wished.

The thing to do is to make a will. If you die without one, your estate will be distributed according to the laws of the state where you lived, not according to your wishes.

Trusts

One way to preserve an estate is with a trust. People use trusts to accomplish a variety of goals. For example, you can set aside money for minor children, make gifts to charity, protect a business, or assure a lifelong income for a spouse.

There are two basic types of trusts, those that are in effect when you are alive (living trust) and those that become effective upon your death (testamentary trust).

A testamentary trust is created by a will and administered by the Probate Court. In this type of trust the transfer of the estate's assets are made only at the death of the trustor.

A living trust can be irrevocable, in which you permanently give up control, or revocable, in which you are allowed to change the provisions or rescind the trust entirely. If a trust is irrevocable, it is not a part of your estate, since you have given the assets away. Before you set up a trust, decide what you want it to accomplish and then talk to an attorney about establishing one.

If you establish a trust, you will have to name a trustee to administer it according to your instuctions. There have been cases in which an individual was the trustee, and assets of the trust were misused or stolen. So it's probably better to name a bank as the trustee. If a bank employee violates the trust, presumably the bank will restore the money.

LIFETIME INVESTMENTS

Many people cultivate a lifelong habit of investing. These are the people who regularly set aside money to achieve their goals. They take charge of their finances and know the difference between the return on a mutual fund and that on a CD.

Unfortunately, other people consider investing as socking away a few hundred dollars in a CD and rolling it over into a new CD when the old one matures. They often spend so much time on not losing money that they seldom think about how to make it. Usually, these are the people who don't understand risk and lack an investment plan.

Develop an Investment Plan

Before you invest, set realistic goals, then develop an investment plan. Once you have a plan, determine how much money you can invest each month to achieve your goals. Investing is similar to taking a trip. First you decide where you want to go and then you plan how you are going to get there.

One purpose of this book is to help you develop your personal investment plan. To get you started, three asset allocation plans were suggested. During your lifetime, your plan could take many detours from what you originally designed. For example, when you have children ready for college, your plan will be different from the one you developed when you were first married.

Determine Your Risk Level

Many investments are risky. Usually, the greater the potential return, the greater the risk. Thus, the main barrier when you invest is the risk factor—the chance that you will lose money. You are the best judge of your tolerance for risk. Once you know your tolerance, use it as a guide when you invest. Regardless of the potential return on an investment, if it makes you uncomfortable, you should consider other investments.

Investment Selections

The list of investment choices in Chapter 2 does not cover every way you can invest. It is confined to investments that are good and those that are risky. The ideal investment has low to moderate risk and provides a good return. Four investment areas have low to moderate risk and the potential to provide a good return:

- Money market mutual funds.
- U.S. government bond funds, corporate and municipal bond funds, and zero-coupon bonds.
- Quality common stocks.
- Pure no-load mutual funds.

10

Questions and Answers About Investing

The following questions and answers include inquiries that have been raised about the DCAP formula and other investment topics covered in this book. No doubt, there will be more questions about the formula when it gains wider acceptance.

Q. Mr. Allen, I'd like to know how long you have been an investor, if you have been successful, and how long you have used the DCAP formula.

A. I've been an investor for over thirty years, and I feel that I've been fairly successful. I've been using the DCAP formula to invest in mutual funds for about three years. I wish I had developed the formula earlier, when I first started to invest. If I had, I'd probably be richer now.

Q. How many mutual funds do you invest in and do you apply the DCAP formula to all of them?

A. I have four growth stock funds, three municipal bond funds, and two money market funds. Before each monthly investment, I apply the DCAP formula to all of the stock funds. I do not apply the formula to the bond and money market funds.

Q. Why don't you use the formula with your bond funds?

A. Because the price of these funds is not volatile enough. Stock funds usually have a greater high/low price range than bond funds. The idea is to invest more when a fund's price is low and level off investments when it is high. I think the formula might work with a bond fund, but the rate of return probably wouldn't be as good as with a stock fund because of the smaller price range.

Q. When and how did you develop the DCAP formula?

A. I began experimenting with the formula about five years ago after I opened an account with the CGM Capital Development Fund. After I had invested in this fund for a couple of years, I felt that I could improve my return if I could only find the right investment approach. As I continued investing in the CGM fund, I recognized that it was well-managed, had volatility, and wasn't a large fund, which is one of my investment criteria. That's when I began to experiment with the formula and developed it to the product you see today. The formula was so successful with the CGM fund that I opened an account with three other funds to apply the formula.

Q. What is your return on the CGM fund?

A. My average annual total return for about five years is about 20 percent, which is good when you consider that CDs are now paying around 4 percent.

Q. Do you invest only in smaller funds? What do you consider a large fund?

A. I consider funds with assets under $500 million as small, and these are the ones I usually invest in. However, I do have one fund with assets over $5 billion, but I bought it specifically to test the formula on a larger fund. Other than its size, this fund meets all my investment criteria.

Q. Why don't you like larger funds?

A. Because of their size, it's difficult for them to take a significant position in smaller stocks. Thus, they may miss out on the growth that many smaller stocks offer.

Q. I'm not sure that I understand the formula when it comes to increasing investments when a fund drops below the target price. Will you explain it?

A. It's easy. Let me explain it in relation to the four growth funds that I invest in each month. After I made my initial investment in these funds, I set a target price. If the net asset value, a fund's price, falls below the target price, I increase the amount of my investment.

For example, when the price of a fund drops 5 percent below its target price, I increase my monthly investment 20 percent. If a fund drops 10 percent below my target price, I increase my investment 40 percent. In other words, for each 5 percent drop in the fund's price, my investment increases 20 percent, but only to a total of 100 percent. So if I am investing $100 a month and the fund's price drops 25 percent, my monthly investment is $200.

The 5 percent figure also works in reverse. This happens when a fund that has dropped, say 25 percent from the target price, stops dropping and goes up in price. In this case, for each 5 percent increase in its price toward the target price, investments are increased 20 percent to a total of 100 percent.

Let me give you an example. Let's say I invest in a fund selling for $20 a share and I set my target price at $20. If the price of the fund drops to $19, my monthly investment increases 20 percent. If the fund's price drops even more to $15, a 25 percent drop from the target price, my monthly investment increases 100 percent, the maximum allowed before investments stop.

Now let's suppose the fund stops dropping and its price goes from $15 to $16. In this situation, I reduce the amount of my monthly investment 20 percent. For each $1 increase in the fund's price, in relation to the target price, the amount of my monthly investment decreases 20 percent, but only to a total of 100 percent since that places me back at $20, which is the target price.

Q. Isn't it expensive to invest by the DCAP formula when monthly investments can increase 100 percent?

A. Not if you have the money. Before I open an account with a fund, I determine if I can afford it. By this, I mean can I afford the minimum initial investment a fund requires, and will I have enough money to invest every month in the fund.

Once I open an account, I invest in the fund every month. After I pay my monthly living expenses, the next payments are to my mutual funds. I believe that the easiest way to gain wealth is by setting aside money each month for investments.

Q. Mr. Allen, which financial publications do you read?

A. I subscribe to *Forbes, Business Week, Investor's Business Daily*, and a newsletter, the *Chartist*. In addition, I occasionally buy *Money, Barron's*, and *Fortune* at the newsstand.

Q. Do you find these publications helpful when you invest in mutual funds?

A. Yes and no. *Forbes* and *Business Week* issue an annual ranking of funds where I get some ideas. *Investor's Business Daily* includes a section on funds that is quite helpful. I subscribe to these publications mainly because I also invest in stocks. The information they provide on funds is a bonus to me.

Q. Do you use the formula when you invest in stocks?

A. Not yet, although I have bought two or three stocks and averaged down. That is, when the price of the stocks dropped, I purchased more shares to reduce my average price per share. This is similar to using the formula. I'm experimenting with the formula to invest in stocks, but I feel it may have to be revised to accommodate them. I'm not saying the formula won't work with stocks; in fact, I think it will. It's that with stocks the risk would be greater, especially with only one stock. In fact, with only one stock, you could conceivably lose your entire investment. If the formula were used with a portfolio of stocks, say five to ten, it would work better than with only one.

Q. I'm not sure I agree with you that a discount broker is better than a full-service broker. I'm the type of person who needs all the help I can get when I invest. Wouldn't a full-service broker be better for me?

A. Whether you use a discount or a full-service broker is your decision. However, if you need investment help, you can get that from publications as well as from a full-service broker. Full-service brokers are salespeople who work on a commission or a salary plus commission basis. So the more they sell, the more they earn. My feeling is that if you want to do some serious investing, you must think and act by yourself. I'm not saying that full-service brokers are not sincere when it comes to investment advice, but they are salespeople, and the amount of their income is directly related to their sales volume. So you figure it out.

Q. Mr. Allen, can I have your ideas on investing in individual stocks?

A. Certainly. Buy low and sell high or buy high and sell higher. And that's easier said than done. Seriously, I rely more on technical rather than fundamental analysis when I select stocks. Technical analysis involves interpreting charts and relative strength to predict the price movement of a stock, while fundamental analysis is concerned with a company's balance sheet and income statement for predicting the movement of a stock. Although I rely more on technical analysis, I also check a stock's fundamentals before I invest.

Also, I spend a lot of time watching the tickertape of the New York and NASDAQ stock exchanges. I make decisions to buy stocks based on the action I observe on these tapes. I exclude the American Stock Exchange because of a lack of time.

I rely a lot on my computer. I use it to get stock prices, charts, technical analysis, and company reports. Also, I buy and sell stocks in my office with my computer.

Q. Do you invest in any specific stock groups?

A. I follow all the stock groups at one time or another. I am primarily a trend follower, so I usually invest in those groups that are rising in price. As you probably know, stocks are in and out of favor. One month, the utility stocks may go up in price. The next month, durable goods stocks and then the computer stocks rise, so I try to follow the groups that are rising in price.

I have done very well investing in oversold electric utility stocks. Of course, these stocks were not in favor when I bought them. In fact, they were completely out of favor. That's one reason I bought them. So I suppose you could also call me a contrarian.

Q. Will you put names on the utility stocks?

A. Allegheny Power Systems, Nipsco Industries, Niagara Mohawk Power, Tucson Electric Power, and El Paso Electric. I made a good profit when I sold Allegheny and Nipsco. I still own the other three utility stocks.

Q. What do you mean by a good profit?

A. When I sold these stocks, my return was over 300 percent on both of them.

Q. Aren't Tucson and El Paso down considerably from their high price, and aren't they risky investments?

A. It's true these utilities are way off their high price for the last few years, but I bought them near their lows. In response to your second question, I don't feel they are overly risky, at least not for my investment program. I like to swing for the long ball, try to hit a home run. Moreover, I can't imagine the cities of Tucson and El Paso without electricity. Some day these utilities are going to come back in price.

The caveat with the two utilities concerns the time value of money. In other words, would other investments provide me a greater return than these utilities during the same period? If it takes a long time for them to turn around and become profitable, then I would have a greater return with other investments.

Q. Isn't it a lot of work to keep track of stocks and watch the ticker tape the way you do?

A. Nothing is really work unless you would rather be doing something else. I enjoy investing.

Q. Are there any other electric utility stocks that you are thinking about investing in?

A. I've looked at Public Service of New Mexico, but I haven't decided if I'll invest in the company.

Q. How did you look at Public Service of New Mexico?

A. I wrote for the company's annual report, checked its earnings per share, included it as one of the stocks I chart on my computer, and read articles about the company.

Q. With the four funds that you own, how did you determine where to set the target price?

A. I set all of my funds' target prices when I make my initial investment. I set it on the basis of their historical price range, covering a period that includes both up and down market cycles. When I include both cycles, it shows how management has performed in bull and bear markets. If a fund has had a management change during the period, I take this into account. In this situation, I determine the target price from the time the last management took charge of the fund. That's because I don't care what the previous management did. What I'm concerned with is the performance of the present management.

Q. When is the best time to make an initial investment in a fund?

A. Any time that you have the money. However, some people advise not to invest just before a fund makes a distribution. This is because you pay taxes on the distribution without the benefit of having owned the fund for any length of time before the distribution. I'm not sure I accept the advice of these people. Certainly, a fund holder has to pay taxes on distributions, but whether to invest before a distribution also depends on the action of the fund around the time of the distribution. For example, if a fund is rising in price at distribution time, it could be better to invest prior to the distribution to participate in the fund's increase in price. Most funds make their distributions in December. So, if you agree with the distribution theory, January might be the best time to make your initial investment.

Q. **Do you always reset your funds' target price after a distribution, and can the target price guarantee profits?**

A. No, I only reset the target price when a distribution plus any change in the fund's price results in a new high or low for the fund.

The setting and resetting of a target price will not guarantee profits. In the short term, you can set and reset the target price, and the value of your fund can still be lower than your average cost per share. However, over the long term you should come out ahead, especially if you select a good fund and use the DCAP formula.

Q. **Mr. Allen, are you saying that even when I use the target price to control the flow of money to a fund, there may be years when the amount I invest will be more than what the shares are worth?**

A. That's correct. Investing in mutual funds is not an exact science such as physics. Mutual funds should be considered as long-term investments, and over the long term many funds have provided some very good returns.

Q. **How much money should I have before I develop my asset allocation plan and begin investing—about $2,000?**

A. No, not nearly that much money. You can have an asset allocation plan and begin investing with as little as $100, $50 for an initial investment in a growth fund and $50 for some type of money market fund. Of course, $100 isn't much money, but no matter how small the amount in your asset allocation plan, it is a start. Getting started is the important thing. After you start, follow up with monthly investments to both your mutual and money market funds.

One way to acquire wealth is to invest on a monthly basis. Investing monthly gets you in the habit of saving, and it may surprise you how much you can save if you really try. Of course, if you want to save even more, cut back on nonessential expenses and invest the money.

Q. **Mr. Allen, it seems to me that you are of the opinion that money can buy happiness. Is that true?**

A. No, money doesn't buy happiness. Nor does poverty buy it. But money does make for financial independence. To be independent requires that you have money saved for emergencies, adequate life and health insurance, and some investments.

Q. You recommend that mutual funds be checked every month to see how they are performing. Isn't that too often? Wouldn't once a year be as good?

A. I've always felt that mutual funds should be given a checkup every month. Frequent checkups are important if you are a beginner investor because they get you acquainted with the action of your fund. Also, when you invest by the DCAP formula, you should check the price of your fund monthly to see if the target price needs to be reset and to determine the amount of your investment.

In addition, if you own stocks, you should review them daily. At times, such as when you are traveling, it's difficult to look at your stocks each day. In this situation, you can tell your broker to place stop loss orders on your stocks. Stop loss orders instruct your broker to sell your stocks once a given price is attained either on the up or down side. Stop orders can reduce the pressure of investing, especially when you can't check the daily action of your stocks.

Q. About how much should I have in a fund for emergency situations?

A. It's difficult to put a dollar amount on it because it depends on your family situation. Usually, an amount equal to three or four months of your net income is adequate. If you are single with no dependents, you shouldn't need as much in an emergency fund as someone who has three dependents. The purpose of an emergency fund is to pay for the small unforeseen expenses so you won't have to draw on your other investments. It's surprising how the cost of little things can wreck an investment plan.

Q. Because of risk, I invest only in CDs. I have $10,000 in them. I just can't bring myself to invest in stocks or even

mutual funds. Do you have any suggestions on how I can start investing in mutual funds?

A. Yes. Heroes are made and not born. This means that to be successful you must try new approaches. You say because of risk you invest only in CDs. Yet CDs are one of the riskiest investments. That's because they carry the risk that inflation will erode their return. For example, let's say you get 4 percent on your CDs, inflation is 4 percent a year, and you are in a 28 percent tax bracket. In this case, after you pay taxes on the interest earned on the CDs, you are actually receiving a minus return. The trouble with inflation is that it is insidious. You may think you are receiving a fair return with your CDs, but you are actually losing money when inflation is considered.

I'd suggest that you withdraw $1,000 of your CD money and invest it in a growth fund. I advise $1,000 because it's not a relatively large amount and most funds require a $1,000 minimum initial investment.

Before you invest in a fund, do your homework. Go to the library and read about mutual funds. Get the telephone number of some funds and call for a prospectus. Compare the average annual return, fees, services, and investment philosophy of several funds. On the basis of your comparison, select the fund that meets your investment objectives.

Invest every month in the fund that you select. Keep a record of your investments and all distributions paid by the fund. After you invest in the fund for a year, look at its total return. Compare the return with what you could have earned if you had kept your $1,000 in a CD. If your fund's return is less than what you could have earned with a CD, don't get discouraged. The big money in mutual funds is made by investing for the long term.

Continue investing in your fund, and, at the end of each year, calculate its return and compare it with the return on a CD. If you selected a good fund, it won't be long before you'll see that your fund is providing a greater return than what you could have earned on a CD.

Q. I've been an investor for several years and have an asset allocation plan that contains $10,000 in two bank CDs, a

$1,000 emergency fund, and five hundred shares of Westinghouse common stock that I bought at $31 a share. Do you think this is a good mix for my asset allocation plan?

A. No. Let's start with Westinghouse. Westinghouse has recently had to experience writeoffs, layoffs, and selloffs, and the price of its stock has been battered down to reflect this. Unless there is more bad news about Westinghouse, I'd hold the stock and maybe buy more to reduce your average cost per share. I think the stock price has stabilized and someday Westinghouse will sell at a much higher level.

As for the CDs, I think you know my feelings about them. Their rate of return is too low compared to other types of investments. If you must have CDs, then buy them through a broker, such as Charles Schwab, where the yield is about 0.5 percent to 1 percent higher than at a bank. You can often sell your CDs back to the broker before maturity, usually without paying a penalty that a bank would charge. I'd also suggest that you sell one of your CDs and put the money in a growth and income fund.

Q. The asset allocation plans in your book seem conservative to me. I like a little more excitement in my investment portfolio, so what do you suggest?

A. First, you didn't say what holdings are in your portfolio. Second, the asset allocation plans are offered only to give you ideas on how you can shape your portfolio. The investments in a portfolio will vary among individuals. If you want to juice up your portfolio, then put a larger percent of your assets in common stocks. If you do add stocks to your portfolio, follow them closely. To give you an idea of how much stocks can fall in price, in 1992, Westinghouse sold as high as $39 a share. Look at it now, it's around $13. In 1992, IBM sold as high as $175. Where is it now?

One thing to remember: No stock should be considered as a permanent investment. You can't buy stocks and forget about them. If you own stocks, they need to be reviewed daily. And if they begin to perform poorly, sell them.

Q. How does one know when to sell a stock?

A. There is no set formula on when to sell a stock. For me, it's much easier to know when to buy a stock than when to sell one. Some people recommend that investors put an upside price to sell a stock. For example, if you buy a stock at $25, set an upside price of $35 when it should be sold. I don't like this approach to investing. If the stock was a good buy at $25, maybe it's an even better buy at $35. It's okay to sell the stock at $35 if it's not performing as well as the general market, its sales and earnings are decreasing, or it looks weak on a technical basis.

Since I am primarily a technical analyst, I would look at the chart of the $35 stock. As it rose in price from $25 to $35, it developed price support levels (the price level at which buyers have tended to purchase a stock in volume, thus overcoming the downward pressure from sellers of the stock). If it appears that the stock is going to break through the first price support, I'd sell it. Several reasons could cause a stock to break through a support level, all of them bad.

First, the general market could be in a decline, which means that almost all stocks will follow the market. If it's the beginning of a bear market, a market with descending prices, few stocks go unscathed. In this case, it's better to have your dollars in a money market fund and reenter the market when prices turn up.

Second, the stock could be experiencing an earnings problem. That is, either its earnings have gone down or they are expected to go down. In either case, a real or expected earnings decline usually hammers the price of a stock.

And last, other factors such as a decline in the stock's product sales, internal problems with management, or new technology could send the stock's price down.

When I buy a stock, I set a 10 percent limit as the amount of loss I will tolerate if it drops in price. For instance, if I buy a stock at $20 and it falls to $18, I usually sell it. This strategy preserves most of my money for another investment. Since I started investing, this is probably the most important strategy I've used. There is usually no reason to hold a stock that has dropped more than 10 percent from the purchase price. It should be sold to save most of your money for other investments.

Q. Mr. Allen, what is the most important thing to consider when I screen funds for investment purposes, and what is a good return for a fund?

A. By far, the most important selection criteria is the fund's past performance in both up and down market cycles. A good return would be a fund that has an average annual total return of 14 percent or better since its inception. Anything less than 12 percent is unacceptable.

Q. How can I get information on the many fees that some funds charge their shareholders?

A. Since a fund must disclose all its fees in its prospectus, that's where to get the information. Remember, funds can impose front-end loads, back-end loads, 12b-1 fees, and management and customer service fees. Not all these fees are charged by most funds, but in recent years there has been an increase in the amount and number of fees. When you receive a prospectus, add up the different fees and use it as a reference when comparing funds.

The puzzling question is why some funds have such high fees while others have reasonable fees. I suppose the answer is greed and a generally uninformed public. As I have said several times, there is simply no reason to invest in a fund that has charges other than management and customer service fees.

Q. Mr. Allen, do you think it is better to invest in a fund that is part of a family of funds or an independent type fund?

A. There is nothing wrong with investing in a fund that is not a part of a family of funds. Many independent type funds have turned in good performances. The advantages to investing in a fund that is part of a family are that you can switch to other funds within the family and they almost always have a money market fund that may be handy.

Q. **Where is the best place to buy shares in a fund, to make my initial investment?**

A. Directly from the fund. You could use the services of a full-service broker, financial adviser, insurance agent, or bank. But if you use one of these, be prepared to pay a commission.

Q. **I have invested my IRA money in a money market fund. Do you think this is a wise investment, or should I put some of my IRA in other types of investments?**

A. It depends a lot on your risk tolerance. If it doesn't make you uneasy, I'd suggest that you put some of your IRA money in investments such as stock and bond funds.

Q. **My bank wants me to roll over my maturing CDs into a mutual fund it sponsors. Is this a good deal?**

A. Absolutely not. Bank-managed mutual funds are virtually all front-end load funds. In addition, they may charge 12b-1 and back-end load fees. Until banks can come up with lower fees, stay away from them.

Glossary of Investment Terms

Account. A bookkeeping record of a client's transactions with an investment firm. It includes a client's credit and debit balances of cash and securities.

Annuitant. A person who receives benefits from an annuity.

Annuity. An investment contract sold by a life insurance company. The annuitant receives payments for life or a fixed period in exchange for a one-time payment or fixed-period installments of money.

Asset. Any item of value owned by an individual or corporation.

Ask price. The net asset value (NAV) plus any sales charge of a mutual fund.

Automatic reinvestment plan (ARP). An option available to mutual fund shareholders by which their dividends and capital gains are reinvested to buy additional shares.

Automatic withdrawal. An option available to mutual fund shareholders that allows them to receive a fixed dollar amount of their assets periodically.

Average annual total return. The total of a mutual fund's price increase or decrease plus dividends and interest for one year, expressed as a percentage of increase or decrease.

Back-end load. A fee charged by a mutual fund when a shareholder redeems shares.

Balance sheet. A financial statement that shows a company's assets, liabilities, cash, debt, and other data on a particular date.

Bankers' acceptance. A short-term non–interest bearing note sold at discount and redeemed at full value at maturity.

Bear market. A period when stock prices are going down, usually for an extended period of time; the opposite of a bull market.

Bond. A debt security in the form of a loan from the bondholder to a corporation or municipality. The bondholder receives interest payments on the loan.

Broker (stockbroker). A person or firm that acts as an intermediary between buyers and sellers of securities.

Bull market. A period when stock prices are going up, usually for an extended period of time; the opposite of a bear market.

Capital appreciation. An increase in the value of an asset, such as stocks, bonds, mutual funds, and other types of investments. Also called appreciation.

Capital gains. The profit from the sale of an asset.

Capital loss. The loss from the sale of an asset.

Certificate of deposit (CD). A certificate issued for money deposited in a bank for a specified period of time at a specific rate of interest.

Closed-end fund. A managed investment fund with a fixed number of shares traded in the securities markets through brokers.

Commercial paper. Unsecured promissory notes issued by corporations to provide them with short-term financing.

Commission. A fee charged by a broker for buying and selling securities for an individual or investment firm.

Common stock. Securities that represent ownership in a company, issued in units of shares.

Conversion privilege. The right of a mutual fund shareholder to switch from one fund to another.

Corporate bond fund. A mutual fund that invests primarily in the bonds of corporations.

Corporation. A business organization chartered by a state to conduct business within the state.

Custodian. An organization that holds investments for safekeeping. All IRAs and Keogh plans require a custodian. See fiduciary.

Deep discount bond. A bond that was issued at par value but sells below 80 percent of par value.

Discount broker. A brokerage firm that handles buy and sell orders from customers and charges lower commissions than a full-service broker. See full-service broker.

Distributions. Dividends, interest, and capital gains paid to mutual fund shareholders.

Diversification. A method of investing that involves buying several securities to reduce risk.

Dividend. A payment by a company in the form of cash, stock, or assets to its shareholders.

Dollar-cost averaging. A method of investing equal amounts at regular intervals.

Dollar-Cost Averaging Plus (DCAP). A formula for investing varying amounts in an open-end mutual fund.

Dow-Jones averages. A measure of stock market price movements based on thirty industrials, twenty transportation, and fifteen utility stocks.

Earnings per share. The net income of a company based on the total shares outstanding; computed by dividing the share outstanding by the net earnings.

Equities. Stocks, real estate, and other assets that an investor owns, but not bonds, since an investor lends money for their purchase.

Expense ratio. A ratio of annual expenses to average net assets of a mutual fund.

Family of funds. A group of mutual funds, each having a different investment objective, but managed by the same investment company. A family usually consists of stock, bond, and money market funds.

Fiduciary. A corporation or person entrusted with the control of assets for the benefit of others. Custodians under the Uniform Gifts to Minors Act are considered fiduciaries since they cannot use entrusted assets for their own benefit.

Fixed-income funds. A mutual fund that invests primarily in bonds and preferred stocks.

401(K). A tax-deferred employee retirement plan provided by an employer.

Front-end load. A sales charge that investors pay when buying shares of some mutual funds. See no-load mutual fund.

Full-service broker. A broker who handles buy and sell orders, research, and other services for clients. See discount broker.

GNMA fund. A mutual fund that invests primarily in debt securities of the Government National Mortgage Association.

Government securities. Generic name for U.S. government securities which include treasury bills, notes, and bonds; Series EE bonds; certificates of indebtedness for interbank and interagency transfers of funds; and agency securities such as Federal National Mortgage Association (FNMA) and Government National Mortgage Association (GNMA).

Growth fund. A mutual fund that invests primarily in the common stock of companies whose sales and earnings are expanding. These funds tend to invest in stocks that are expected to increase in value as opposed to those that pay a relatively high dividend.

Growth and income fund. A mutual fund that invests in the common stock of established companies that have increasing share value and a record of paying relatively high dividends.

Growth stock. The common stock of a company whose sales and earnings are increasing in value at a relatively rapid rate.

Index. A measurement of stock market price movement. Examples are Dow-Jones Industrial Average, Standard and Poor's 500, and NASDAQ Index.

Index fund. A mutual fund with a portfolio of securities that includes many of the same stocks as those in an index such as Dow-Jones, Standard and Poor's 500, or NASDAQ.

Individual Retirement Account (IRA). A tax-deferred retirement plan for employed persons.

Inflation. An increase in the selling cost of goods and services resulting in a decrease in the value of what a dollar will buy of these goods and services.

Institutional investor. An investor such as a mutual fund pension fund or a bank with a large investment account.

Interest. Money paid to a lender by a borrower for the use of the money.

Interest rate. The rate of payment, expressed as a percentage, to the lender of the money by the borrower of the money.

Investment adviser. A person or organization that provides advice on investments for a fee.

Investment company. A corporation, trust, or partnership that invests the pooled money of shareholders in securities according to investment objectives. A mutual fund is an investment company.

Investment objective. The investment goal of an individual or investment company.

Junk bonds. Speculative bonds with an investment rating of BB or lower by Standard and Poor's.

Keogh plan. A retirement investment program for self-employed persons.

Leverage. The use of borrowed money, usually from a brokerage firm, to purchase stocks and other types of investments.

Limited partnership. An investment group consisting of a general partner who manages the investment of the partnership. Limited partners usually receive a fixed rate of return, and any loss is limited to the amount they contribute to the partnership.

Load fund. A mutual fund that charges a fee, usually between 2 percent and 8.5 percent, when shares are purchased in the fund. See no-load mutual fund.

Management company. An investment company that directs the operations of a mutual fund; also called an investment adviser.

Market timing. Buying and selling securities at the beginning and end of stock market cycles.

Maturity date. A specific date when the borrower of money is required to repay the principal amount of a debt.

Money market mutual fund. A fund that invests in short-term securities such as certificates of deposit, commercial paper, government securities, and banker' acceptances.

Municipal bond fund. An open-end mutual fund or unit trust that invests in tax-exempt bonds issued by state, city, and local governments.

Mutual fund. An investment company that pools money from investors so that it can be more conveniently, economically, and efficiently managed and invested in securities.

NASDAQ. Acronym for the National Association of Security Dealers Automated Quotations. NASDAQ provides price and volume figures on securities traded on the over-the-counter market.

Net asset value (NAV). The price per share of a mutual fund, determined by dividing the number of shares outstanding into the net assets of a fund.

New York Stock Exchange. The largest and oldest stock exchange in the United States.

No-load mutual fund. A mutual fund that does not have a sales charge, such as a front-end commission. See also load fund.

Open-end fund. A managed investment company (mutual fund) that does not have a fixed number of shares. Shares of open-end companies are sold and redeemed on investor's demand.

Over-the-counter. A market where securities that are not traded on any exchange, such as the New York Stock Exchange, are bought and sold at bid and ask prices.

Payment date. The date when either a stock dividend or interest will be paid by the issuer.

Penny stock. A stock that usually sells for less than $1 and is considered very risky.

Periodic payment plan. A contractual plan for investing in mutual funds. The investor makes payments to a fund on a monthly, quarterly, or other basis.

Portfolio. The total investment holdings of an individual or an investment company.

Portfolio manager. Professional mutual fund or other investment company manager who makes buy and sell decisions on securities according to stated objectives.

Price range. The high and low prices of a security or mutual fund for a specified period, often called a trading range.

Prime rate. Preferential rate of interest charged by banks on short-term loans to their most creditworthy customers, expressed as a percentage.

Prospectus. The official booklet required by the Securities and Exchange Commission that describes a mutual fund's objectives, policies, restrictions, and other information.

Pure no-load mutual fund. A mutual fund that does not have a front-end load, back-end load, or a 12b-1 fee.

Redemption fee. See back-end load.

Reinvestment privilege. See automatic reinvestment plan (ARP).

Return on investment. The percentage gain or loss on an investment.

Risk. The chance that all or part of a person's investment money will be lost.

Sales charge. A commission charged to purchase shares in mutual funds, unit trusts, and limited partnerships. See front-end load.

Sector fund. A mutual fund that invests primarily in one industry.

Securities. Stocks, bonds, warrants, options, and other investments.

Securities and Exchange Commission (SEC). The federal agency established to protect investors.

Shareholder. A person or legal entity that owns common or preferred stock in a corporation, or shares in a mutual fund.

Simplified employee pension (SEP) plan. A retirement plan that combines the features of an IRA and a Keogh plan.

Signature guarantee. A document that verifies the identity of a shareholder or person.

Standard and Poor's 500. A measure of the value change of five hundred common stocks. The S&P 500 is used as a comparison for stock market performance.

Target price. An arbitrary price set by mutual fund shareholders to calculate the amount of monthly investments when using the DCAP formula.

Tax-deferred. The delayed payment of a tax liability on investments such as IRAs and certain annuities.

Tax-exempt securities. Generally refers to municipal bonds issued by state, city, and local governments.

Tickertape. An electronic board that displays the price and volume of securities transactions.

Total financial plan. An investment program that covers all the financial needs of an individual or family.

Total return. A performance calculation that includes the change in an investments value plus any dividends and capital gains, expressed as a percentage.

Transactions. The buying and selling of securities.

Treasury bill. Short-term debt obligation issued by the U.S. government that matures in three months, six months, or one year.

Treasury bond. Long-term debt obligation issued by the U.S. government that matures in ten to thirty years.

Treasury note. Debt obligation of the U.S. government maturing in one to ten years.

Turnover ratio. A measurement of the extent that a mutual fund buys and sells securities.

12b-1 fee. A charge that some mutual funds assess to cover marketing and distribution expenses.

Uniform Gifts to Minors Act. Legislation that allows someone of legal age to serve as custodian for a minor's assets.

Variable annuity. A life insurance contract with a portfolio of securities and debt instruments.

Volatility. The measure of a security's or stock market's price movement.

Volume. The number of shares of stocks and bonds traded during a specific time period.

Yield. Income on an investment expressed as a percentage.

Zero-coupon bonds. A debt security issued at a discount from its face value. No actual interest is paid until maturity.

Index